# Flying Tigers: Chennault in China

P9-DCC-086

# Flying Tigers:
# Chennault in China

Ron Heiferman

Editor-in-Chief: Barrie Pitt
Editor: David Mason
Art Director: Sarah Kingham
Picture Editor: Robert Hunt
Cover: Denis Piper
Special Drawings: John Batchelor
Photographic Research: Jonathan Moore
Cartographer: Richard Natkiel

ISBN 0-345-27899-2

Manufactured in the United States of America

First Edition: December 1971
Second Printing: November 1978

# Contents

# Introduction

Shortly after the Japanese invasion of Manchuria in 1931, the Chinese government took measures to prepare against a Japanese attack on China proper. High ranking German army officers, forced into retirement because of the dismemberment of the Imperial German Army after Versailles, were recruited to retrain Chinese military forces while, at the same time, an American mission was invited to re-form and expand the Chinese Air Force. Headed by Colonel John Jouett, a retired protegé of General Billy Mitchell, the American Air Mission undertook to rebuild the Chinese Air Force into an effective unit capable of warding off a Japanese attack. Between 1932 and 1934, Jouett and the nine pilots who accompanied him established the nucleus of what could have been an effective defensive force.

When Jouett arrived in China he found the Chinese Air Force in a state of chaos. There were few aerodromes and bases, fewer airworthy planes, and, worst of all, hardly any pilots capable of flying what few craft the Chinese Air Force could muster. Immediately setting out to rectify this situation, Jouett and his assistants established the Central Chinese Aviation Academy at Hangchow where some 350 pilots were trained to fly 250 new aircraft purchased for the Chinese government by Jouett and his colleagues in Europe and the United States. Unfortunately, the Jouett mission, which had accomplished much during its brief tenure, was abruptly concluded as a result of Japanese pressure and Sino-American political differences.

Following the departure of the American Air Mission in 1934, Italian advisers replaced the Americans in the Chinese Air Force. At the invitation of Generalissimo Chiang Kai-shek, Mussolini dispatched an official mission of forty pilots and a hundred

**Chinese soldiers undergo retraining by redundant German officers**

Colonel (here Major) John Jouett headed
the US group brought in to update the
Chinese Air Force

Generalissimo Chiang Kai-shek ; he
invited Italians to take over from
Jouett's mission

mechanics and engineers to China in 1935. They proceeded to establish a flying school at Loyang and a Fiat aircraft assembly plant in Nanchang. Although American civilians continued to operate the Hangchow academy, they were quickly eclipsed by the Italians, who not only trained large numbers of Chinese air cadets but also profited from millions of dollars worth of aircraft purchased by the Chinese government. On the eve of the Japanese invasion of China in 1937, the Italians were in full control of the Chinese Air Force.

In April 1937, less than three months before the Marco Polo Bridge incident, the Chinese government invited Claire Chennault to undertake a three month survey of the Chinese Air Force. Chennault, a controversial

**Mme Chiang, flanked by her protégé Claire Chennault and the Generalissimo**

**Shanghai, 1937; the Japanese assault on China leaves in its wake scenes of tragedy destined to become commonplace in the following years**

proponent of aerial warfare, retired from the United States Army Air Force on a medical discharge to undertake this important mission at the insistence of Madame Chiang Kai-shek. Madame Chiang, who had been designated by her husband to oversee the development of China's air defences, had heard of Chennault and his controversial policies through some of her American acquaintances and quickly accepted their suggestion that Chennault be commissioned to render an impartial report on the combat-readiness of the Italian trained Chinese Air Force.

Chennault left for China on 1st May, 1937 beginning a career which, unknown to him at the time, would keep

him in China until 1945 and the war's end. At the time, however, his plan was to complete his review and return home. During May and June 1937, Chennault inspected Chinese Air Force facilities and training centres. His observations during this period led him to the conclusion that the Chinese Air Force was hopelessly unprepared to effectively defend China against a Japanese attack. Under Italian tutelage, the Chinese Air Force had grown markedly in size but, as Chennault readily observed, the quality of men in the Air Force and the equipment they were forced to use left much to be desired. Chennault was particularly critical of the Italian Flying School at Loyang which graduated all cadet entrants regardless of whether or not they could fly. Since most of these cadets were drawn from the families of the wealthy supporters of the Kuomintang (KMT) and constituted an élite social corps, the Italian practice of indiscriminately graduat-

**Polikarpov I-153 in China; Russia supplies aircraft and instruction**

12

A Claude, precursor of the brilliant Zero; Japanese training and machines quickly prove superior to Chinese air power

ing all cadet entrants was pleasing to Chiang Kai-shek, who was unaware of how poorly trained the large number of Chinese aviators were and assumed that they were competent flyers. Tragically, the performance of the Chinese Air Force immediately following the Japanese invasion revealed the shortcomings of these cadets and their training.

Chennault was preparing his report on the Chinese Air Force when the Japanese engineered the Marco Polo Bridge incident as a pretext for their invasion of China in July 1937. The Japanese offensive was swift and decisive. Despite the heroic resistance of Chinese defence forces in certain areas, the Japanese quickly captured urban centres along the China coast

and were rapidly proceeding along the Yangtze river as the Chinese government retreated westward.

At the outset of the Sino-Japanese conflict, air combat on both sides was poorly executed. It soon became clear, however, that the Chinese Air Force was incapable of blunting the Japanese advance along the Yangtze and powerless to defend the country from Japanese aerial attacks. Although the Chinese possessed some 500 aircraft at the outset of the war, only ninety-one of these were airworthy and few of the air cadets were fit for combat. As a result, the Japanese wrested control of the skies over China from the Chinese during the first weeks of the war and for three years thereafter used China as an aerial laboratory in which Japanese pilots gained valuable combat experience. During the early years of the war China was used as a training

**Devastating attacks on Chungking open the Japanese air offensive in southwest China. The formation of the AVG is a direct result**

theatre for Japanese pilots who flew from land and carrier bases. As a result of such opportunities, on the eve of the attack on Pearl Harbor, Japanese pilots were collectively perhaps the most experienced pilots in the war, surpassing in their efficiency and skill their Axis counterparts in Germany and Italy.

As it became clear that the Chinese Air Force was powerless to defend the country against Japanese attacks, many influential Chinese proposed that an international aerial volunteer unit be formed to defend China. Such an idea was not a new one. Indeed, in 1931, following the Japanese occupation of Manchuria, H H Kung, brother-in-law of Generalissimo Chiang Kai-shek and an important Kuomintang

official, had proposed this idea. At the time, Kung's proposal was tabled by Chiang Kai-shek at the suggestion of Colonel Jouett, head of the American Air Mission, on the ground that such a programme might interfere with the expansion of the Chinese Air Force. In October 1937, however, the situation was different. With their Italian advisers leaving the country because of treaty commitments with the Japanese and only twelve operational aircraft left following the Battle for Shanghai, the Chinese Air Force could hardly offer effective resistance to the Japanese. Therefore, an international air legion was hastily formed to defend the country.

The International Air Squadron was composed of British, Dutch, and American volunteers. Flying aircraft purchased for the Chinese government by American arms merchant William Pawley, these men, some several dozen in number, flew a series of

missions against Japanese installations in North China during the winter of 1937-1938. Unfortunately for the Chinese, this motley collection of men and machines were no match for the Japanese and their activities were quickly brought to an end when the Japanese destroyed their base at Hankow in 1938. Were it not, then, for the arrival of Russian advisers and air units, China would have been totally defenceless against Japanese air raids.

The arrival of six Russian air squadrons in China (two bomber squadrons and four fighter squadrons) shortly after the conclusion of the Sino-Soviet Non-Aggression Pact on 21st August, 1937 allowed the Chinese to re-group their air force in Kunming while, at the same time, providing aerial cover for the Chinese armies and protection against Japanese attacks. The Russian air units sent to China were regular units of the Russian Air Force, commanded by their own officers, and sent to China complete with Russian ground crews and supplies. The Russian pilots were tough, able, well disciplined, and used China as a proving ground for their equipment and tactics. Between 1937 and 1940, they constituted China's most important aerial bulwark against the Japanese.

In addition to the despatch of six squadrons to China, the Russians sent 400 planes there to be used by the Chinese Air Force. In order to train Chinese airmen and cadets in the use of this equipment, several flying and artillery schools were established. The graduates of these schools soon proved to be among China's most effective airmen. It was no accident that the leaders of China's Air Force during the war were almost all Russian trained.

The aerial defence provided by Russian units in China was limited. Despite the efficiency of their operations, they were vastly outnumbered by the Japanese who were able to stalemate the Russians in North China while, at the same time, sending additional units to attack Chinese installations in Szechwan and Yunnan.

In January 1939, the Japanese launched a massive aerial offensive in south-west China beginning with the first air raids on Chungking, the wartime capital of the Chinese government. Designed to break the military stalemate with the Chinese Nationalists and force them into submission, these raids continued unabated for months. The lack of adequate defences against these then allowed the Japanese to bomb at will. Once again, the Chinese Air Force was unable to defend targets against the Japanese. The International Air Squadron, or what remained of it, was ineffective. The Russians were tied down in North China. In short, the situation was critical. To meet it, the American Volunteer Group (AVG) was conceived and formed.

# The American Volunteer Group

As the Japanese relentlessly continued their air raids against Chungking, Claire Chennault, then a colonel in the Chinese Air Force, and Major General Mao Pang-tzo, Director of the Operations Division, Chinese Air Force, were summoned to Chungking by Chiang Kai-shek in October 1940. Chiang proposed that Chennault and Mao undertake a mission to the United States in order to purchase American aircraft and hire American pilots to fly them against the Japanese. Although pessimistic about the possibility of being able to purchase the latest planes in light of the need for such craft in the European war, and sceptical about the efficacy of a new volunteer force in China in light of their experience with the International Air Squadron, Mao and Chennault agreed to undertake the mission and immediately left for the United States.

Arriving in the States in November 1940, Mao and Chennault presented Chiang's proposal to the President's Liaison Committee, the civilian agency coordinating foreign arms purchase in the United States, on 25th November 1940. Chiang's proposal, drawn up with the cooperation of Chennault and Mao, called for the purchase of 660 planes (500 combat planes, 150 training planes, ten transports) and sufficient material for the construction of fourteen major airfields and 122 landing strips plus sufficient ammunition and ordnance for one year's operation. In addition to these requests for equipment, the Generalissimo asked for permission to recruit volunteers in the United States to fly, service and train Chinese pilots to fly the planes purchased.

Officials in Washington DC found Chiang's proposals incredible. Because of the need to supply England with equipment of all varieties so that she could defend herself against the Nazis, and the rapid expansion of

**An AVG pilot runs up the engine of his fearsomely masked P-40**

American military and naval forces then underway, military leaders at the Pentagon initially refused to consider Chiang's plan for assistance. But fortunately for the proponents of the American Volunteer Group, Chennault and Mao found important supporters for their scheme in White House advisers Lauchlin Currie and Thomas Corcoran and Cabinet members Frank Knox, Secretary of the Navy, and Henry Morgenthau, Secretary of the Treasury. Together with T V Soong, Chinese Ambassador to the United States, they were successful in converting President Franklin D Roosevelt in favour of the project, thus clearing away many of the official obstacles in the path of the creation of an American volunteer group.

Given the go-ahead by the White House, Chennault began the arduous task of purchasing aircraft for the new volunteer force. During the winter of 1940-1941, he travelled extensively throughout the United States visiting aircraft factories and military installations. Buying aircraft for the American Volunteer Group proved a most difficult task. The Royal Air Force had been granted first priority to purchase aircraft in the United States, and the United States Navy and Army, then rapidly expanding their air units, had placed orders with domestic producers far exceeding their capacity to manufacture. Thus the likelihood that Chennault would be able to purchase any planes, let alone the 660 that Chiang had ordered, was slim.

Eventually, through the efforts of Burdette Wright, vice-president of the Curtis-Wright Aircraft Corporation, and William D Pawley, an agent of Curtis-Wright in China, a deal was arranged for the purchase of one hundred P-40B fighters, rejected by the British to whom they were consigned by Curtis-Wright. In return for the release of their option to purchase the P-40Bs, the Curtis-Wright Corporation promised to supply the

British with a more advanced version of the fighters. When the British acceded to this arrangement in January 1941, the planes were sold to the Chinese at a cost of $8,900,000.

The P-40B fighter was not the most suitable craft for use in China, but it was the only plane available. All efforts to supplement the original purchase from Curtis-Wright with additional planes, particularly medium bombers, failed. Desperate to obtain whatever equipment they could, the Chinese accepted the P-40s even though the planes had not been properly equipped or prepared for combat. In their haste to obtain them, the Chinese accepted the P-40s on the understanding that the British, to whom these planes were originally destined, would release guns, ammunition, and other equipment from

their lend-lease stocks to finish the fitting out of the planes.

When the British could not or would not complete the fitting out of the hundred planes purchased by the Chinese, China Defence Supplies Inc., the principal purchasing and supply agent for the Chinese government in the United States, argued that if the British could not equip the aircraft, the Department of War of the United States was obliged to do so. Although some officials at the War Department were reluctant to agree with this conclusion and complete the fitting out of the aircraft purchased by the Chinese, Secretary for War Henry L Stimson refused to accede to their suggestion that the War Department was not responsible for equipment purchased for the American Volunteer Group. Although the AVG was not the formal

**American planes swell the depleted ranks of the Chinese Air Force**

responsibility of the War Department or for that matter of the United States Government, Stimson believed that sending the planes to China without ammunition and proper armament could cause an international scandal. He informed President Roosevelt to this effect whereupon Roosevelt ordered the War Department to release the equipment necessary to render the P-40s combat-ready.

By 1st February 1941, the planes were crated on docks in New York for shipment to Rangoon. The delivery of the planes was delayed, however, because of a dispute between the Curtis-Wright Corporation and arms merchant, William Pawley, an agent

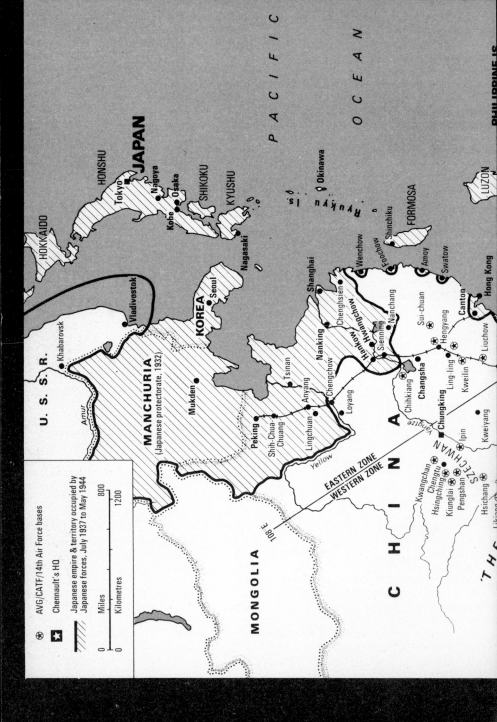

Chennault's bases (AVG, later CATF and 14th Air Force) in China

recruit prospective volunteers on their bases. At a time when both the Army Air Force and the Navy Air Corps were expanding their operations, the formation of the AVG was viewed as a threat to this expansion. Only after Roosevelt issued a presidential directive on 15th April 1941 permitting Chennault and others to recruit members for the AVG on military and naval bases were they prepared to co-operate.

The second complicating factor was the necessity of recruiting pilots and technicians in a manner at least 'legally consistant' with the existing neutrality legislation still in effect between the United States and Japan.

Because of the delicacy of Japanese-American relations, recruitment of the American Volunteer Group had to be carried out with the greatest tact

for Curtis-Wright in China, over payment of a commission on the purchase of the aircraft by the Chinese. The resolution of this dispute took nearly two months, during which time the planes remained in New York at the order of the courts. Only the intervention of Secretary of the Treasury, Henry Morgenthau, on 1st April 1941 broke the deadlock. When both parties in the dispute accepted his compromise solution, the legal obstacle to the shipment of the planes was removed and they were placed on board a Norwegian freighter bound for Burma.

If the procurement of aircraft for the AVG had proved to be a burdensome task, the recruitment of volunteers to fly and service these planes was even more difficult. Two factors complicated the recruiting effort. The first was the reluctance of army and navy commanders to allow agents to

and secrecy. Because America's neutral status with regard to the war in China precluded direct negotiation between the governments of China and the United States over the sale of military hardware or of military assistance, these matters had to be handled by private parties acting with the tacit blessing and support of the Departments of State and War. In this case, the corporations responsible for the transaction between China and the United States were the Central Aircraft Manufacturing Company (CAMCO) and China Defence Supplies. China Defence Supplies acted for the Chinese government in the purchase of planes while CAMCO recruited pilots and mechanics to fly and maintain them.

For official purposes, AVG recruiters were considered employees of CAMCO. Thus, Chennault, designated by the Chinese to lead in American Volunteer Group, bore the non-military title of CAMCO Supervisor while those who volunteered to serve in China were also to be designated as CAMCO employees. Their contracts with CAMCO were masterpieces of evasion. On no occasion was there any public acknowledgement of the war-like nature of the AVG. Those who volunteered to serve in China were offered one year contracts with CAMCO to 'manufacture, repair and operate aircraft'.

From April to July 1941, CAMCO agents toured American air bases recruiting volunteers for the AVG. All the recruiting officers were experienced pilots, returned from the service, and in 'the employ' of CAMCO. At these briefings, conditions of employment were outlined to prospective volunteers. Salaries ranging from $600 to $750 per month plus travelling expenses, living quarters, a supplemental rations allotment of $30 per month, and a paid thirty-day leave were offered to all pilots who volunteered, while mechanics were offered salaries ranging from $150 to $350 per month plus similar fringe

T V Soong, Chinese ambassador to the US, lent his weight to arguments for supplying his country with arms and airmen

benefits. Prospective volunteers would be bound to one-year contracts by CAMCO under which they agreed to serve as agents for the Chinese government. During their time in the AVG, volunteers would retain United States citizenship and, after a year's service in China, they would be free to rejoin their former military units with no loss of rank or service time. In the event of United States entry into the war in Europe or Asia, volunteers would be free to leave China, even if their contracts had not yet expired. Perhaps the most interesting incentive offered to would-be AVG pilots was a $500 bounty (not mentioned in the CAMCO contracts) payed by the Chinese government for each and any confirmed disruption of a Japanese plane.

At each briefing session Chennault

**President Franklin D Roosevelt was persuaded to endorse the aid schemes**

and the other recruiting officers made it clear that the pilots would be participating in a war, but that for purposes of satisfying the fiction of American neutrality, the CAMCO operation was not a military one. All volunteers for the AVG were to be put through a thorough screening by experienced pilots in the employ of CAMCO before they were accepted into the volunteer group. Where possible, only experienced pilots and ground crews were recruited and, theoretically, only men with two years of experience were to be considered for membership in the AVG. In the end, however, reality and ideal did not match. Because of the difficulty of finding volunteers, AVG recruiters were forced to accept men who did not initially meet the criteria for membership originally established by Chennault.

The initial effort to recruit 100 pilots and 150 mechanics was completed in June 1941. In July, the volunteers assembled in San Francisco where they were briefed and they boarded the Dutch liner *Jaegersfontaine* bound for Singapore. Once past the Hawaiian Islands, the liner was escorted through waters near Japanese Mandate Islands in the Pacific by two United States warships until it reached Manila. From Manila, the ship sailed for Singapore where the volunteers boarded a second ship, a Norwegian passenger freighter, bound for Rangoon. The first contingent of the American Volunteer Group reached Rangoon on 28th July 1941, a second contingent followed in September.

According to Chennault's original plan, AVG operations were to be based in Kunming, China. However, due to delays in the shipment of aircraft and the recruitment of personnel and the inability of the Chinese to complete the preparation of the AVG base at Kunming before the onset of the rainy seasons, the first AVG contingent was escorted, instead, to the Kyedaw aerodrome outside Toungoo, Burma. Located 170 miles north of Rangoon, the Kyedaw field with its 4,000-foot asphalt runway was leased to the Chinese for its use as an AVG training centre by the British Colonial Government in Burma and the War Office in London.

Although British authorities generally did their utmost to facilitate American Volunteer Group operations in Burma, the delicacy of Anglo-Japanese relations dictated certain limitations on AVG activities. Since no state of war existed between Britain and Japan, under no circumstances could Kyedaw aerodrome be used to launch attacks on Japanese installations and aircraft. Moreover, in using the base for training, the AVG was to avoid any activities likely to arouse Japanese attention and/or complaints. In addition to the limitations imposed by the diplomatic situation, RAF regulations forbade any alterations of the air base without consent of the chief RAF liaison officer in Burma, Group Captain E R Manning. Manning, who was disturbed by the advent of an irregular air group operating in his command area, adhered scrupulously to regulations and made few concessions to leaders of the AVG.

After their arrival in Rangoon on 28th July 1941, the first contingent of the American Volunteer Group was immediately escorted to the Kyedaw aerodrome by CAMCO agents to begin their orientation and training. For most of these men, this was the first experience that they had had abroad. For those used to living conditions at American military installations in the United States, Kyedaw was a travesty. Totally lacking in creature comforts including screening and electricity and located in an area known for its inhospitable climate, Kyedaw was, as one volunteer put it, 'Burma at its worst'. The uncomfortable realities of living in this hot,

**A Flying Tiger, displays its Chinese Air Force markings**

humid climate quickly took its toll. Despite the presence of three physicians and ample pharmaceutical supplies, malaria · and dysentary soon became part of a way of life. Chennault later learned that the RAF had abandoned the base at Kyedaw because 'Europeans were unable to survive its foul climate'. The AVG was able to survive at Kyedaw for several months, but living on this base sapped the strength and morale of the volunteers.

Training at Kyedaw was a long and arduous process. Although the pilot volunteers possessed experience and the ability to communicate and work together, few of them had extensive experience with fighter aircraft and some had none. The combat techniques they had been taught in the United States were, in Chennault's view, unapplicable in Burma. Therefore, all pilots had to be familiarised with the P-40B fighters they would be flying and introduced to the Chennault air strategy. As Chennault expressed it: 'We began at Toungoo with a kindergarten for teaching bomber pilots how to fly fighters'.

Chennault commenced the AVG combat training course with an introduction to his concept of the use of fighter aircraft. This concept, first defined by Chennault in his book *The Role of Pursuit Aviation*, which was the basic text for all AVG pilots, was based on two suppositions. The first was that fighter planes, when properly used, could easily intercept enemy bombing raids. The second was that bombing missions required fighter protection to avoid heavy losses. Both of these views were considered unorthodox by Chennault's peers

throughout the world of aviation. At a time when almost all airmen viewed the bomber as the weapon of the future and stressed the importance of strategic bombing which they believed could not be seriously hampered by enemy fighters, Chennault was advocating the development of the fighter as an effective weapon.

In his text, Chennault called for development of long-range fighters, adequately armed, and capable of accompanying bombing missions and undertaking strafing runs. More important, he suggested the use of fighters in pairs as opposed to singly in dogfights. Basing his advocacy of paired fighters on the successful practice of German First World War aces, Oswald von Boelcke and Baron Manfred von Richtofen, Chennault suggested that fighter tactics based upon pairs of planes were more effective than individual pursuit or a large

group action. Coupled with effective reconnaissance and Intelligence, Chennault believed this use of fighter aircraft to have great potential.

Although Chennault's views had been dismissed as unrealistic by his colleagues in the United States Air Force, in Burma AVG pilots spent five to eight hours daily mastering his aerial combat theories. On the ground and in the air under battle conditions, AVG pilots put his theories into practice.

Above all, AVG training stressed the importance of teamwork. Heroic individual action was specifically condemned; the men were forced to recognise that teamwork rather than individual heroics was the clue to success. AVG pilots were warned to

27

In Burma CAMCO employees, better known as AVG pilots, collect lunch after a mission

forget the theory of single combat and taught always to fight in pairs with the lead plane moving in for contact while the wing plane protected his tail. Chennault likened each member of the pair to the hand of a boxer who needed two hands to win.

In addition to teamwork, the training programme stressed the absolute necessity for the pilot to know his plane thoroughly, taking advantage of the capabilities of his craft while never letting the enemy take advantage of its weaknesses. The P-40s

flown by AVG pilots were more adequately armed and had more fire power than Japanese fighters, but they were less manoeuvrable. Therefore, although they were particularly effective in diving attacks, in individual pursuit they could not match the Japanese. Chennault often warned his men that if they engaged the Japanese in dogfights reminiscent of the Lafayette Escadrille they would perish. Since pilots and planes were difficult if not impossible to replace, individual heroics and dare-devilry, for which their planes were not suited, could only end in disaster. Although the P40s were far from the best planes in the American arsenal, they were the only planes the AVG had or were likely to get, and they could not afford to lose them unnecessarily.

Having mastered their own equipment, AVG pilots were then subjected to an intensive study of the patterns and habits of Japanese pilots. Chennault had considerable respect for the ability of Japanese pilots and frequently warned his own men that the popular derision of Japanese flyers commonly found among American airmen was not based on fact. Contrary to the impression that the Japanese were second-rate pilots and 'the worst gunners in the world', acting so mechanically that they would not be able to make any man-oeuvre that was not in their flight book, he told them that the Japanese were superb pilots, whose mechanical training and absolute discipline made them dangerous adversaries.

Since the Japanese pilots flew best in large formations, AVG pilots were trained to break up Japanese formations, confronting them with unexpected situations, and exploiting the resulting confusion. Although the Japanese pilots generally lacked the ability to improvise quickly, AVG pilots were warned not to underestimate them, even in this situation.

**Servicing operations continue while Chennault confers with a mechanic**

Chennault trains his fliers to fight in
self-protecting pairs, equivalent to the
German *Rotte,* strategy learned from
First World War German aces

Re-arming and servicing guns. Less manoeuvrable than the best Japanese fighters, the P-40s have to adopt tactics exploiting their greater firepower

Gunnery was also stressed in AVG training so that contacts with the Japanese, though brief, would be lethal. As Chennault pointed out, a fighter plane was nothing more than a gunnery platform and the opportunity to down the enemy came quickly. There was no wasted time. Gunnery training emphasised the conservation of ammunition and supplies. Short bursts were to be used instead of continuous triggering. Pilots were instructed never to fire blindly but, rather, to aim their guns at the most vulnerable spot of the enemy's craft. Thus, for example, when attacking bombers, rather than fire on the whole plane it was expedient to concentrate fire on the planes' gasoline tanks which were inadequately armoured on most Japanese planes. Every bullet had to count. None could be too good at gunnery because an empty gun could mean death.

In simulated combat manoeuvres directed from the ground by Chennault, AVG pilots practiced the techniques they had learned on the ground. After seventy-two hours of classroom lecture, pilots working in pairs spent at least sixty hours performing in the air. Flying at maximum altitudes, travelling in pairs, diving in, making quick passes, and then breaking away from simulated enemy units constituted a daily practice routine, one which AVG pilots mastered with deadly accuracy. In the process, however, equipment losses were heavy. Since the P40s had been purchased with few spare parts, even minor accidents often led to grounding of planes for lack of replacement parts. Thus, when the AVG finally faced the Japanese in actual combat, the number of airworthy craft they could muster was substantially below the original hundred planes purchased by the Chinese.

# Lend-lease to China

Concurrent with the effort to recruit the American Volunteer Group, diplomatic agents of the Chinese government launched an offensive designed to procure American aid for China. The AVG was never meant to be anything more than an expedient temporary effort to provide some air protection against the Japanese until the Chinese Air Force could be equipped and trained to defend their own country. The vehicle to be used for obtaining such equipment was the lend-lease programme.

Although the lend-lease programme had been primarily designed as a device to help the United Kingdom, Chinese officials immediately grasped the programme's significance and applied for lend-lease aid. Early in January 1941, Chiang Kai-shek requested that President Roosevelt send a consultant to China to examine the economic and military situation and prepare a request for lend-lease funds. Roosevelt, acceding to Chiang's request, sent presidential adviser Lauchlin Currie to China late in the month. Currie visited China from 28th January to 4th March 1941. Upon his return to the United States, which coincidentally fell on the very day (11th March 1941) that Congress approved the lend-lease act, Currie was appointed by Roosevelt to serve as co-ordinator of lend-lease aid to China.

In Washington lend-lease to China was heartily supported by an ardent, articulate, and adroit Sinophillic faction which claimed that the Chinese were courageously and competently resisting the Japanese and needed only arms, particularly aircraft, to drive them into the sea. Although military leaders at the Pentagon were too sceptical to accept this view, they too hoped that if the Chinese were rearmed, reorganised, and retrained, they might cause the Japanese sufficient concern as to

T V Soong and Cordell Hull, lend-lease signatories

prevent them from embarking on any adventure in the Pacific. Thus, myth and hope coincided and the lend-lease programme to China was begun.

On 15th March 1941, four days after the United States Congress passed the lend-lease act, President Roosevelt announced the beginning of lend-lease aid to China and the Chinese were invited to submit their requests. On 31st March, T V Soong, Chinese Ambassador to the United States, presented Chiang Kai-shek's proposals. The programme suggested by the Chinese called for a major enlargement of the Chinese Air Force. Whereas the Mao-Chennault programme envisaged the purchase of 660 aircraft, Soong now called on the United States to supply 1,000 planes to the Chinese Air Force, plus supplies of replacement parts and American Air advisers to train Chinese personnel to use them. In view of the fact that Chennault had only been able to procure a hundred planes for the AVG between November 1940 and January 1941 (and then only as a result of manipulations of consignments to England) Soong's proposals might have seemed outrageous were it not for two facts. Firstly, President Roosevelt had publicly stated that the defence of China was vital to American interests earlier in the month (i.e. March 1941). Secondly, the lend-lease programme, which had not been approved by Congress when Chennault made his initial proposal, was now operating. Therefore, when Soong presented his proposals for lend-lease aid, he had reason to believe that his request might be fulfilled in part, if not in full.

Currie presented Soong's proposals to the War Department in April, 1941. At the Pentagon the requests were criticised as being too general. It was believed that the Chinese were not prepared to take full advantage of lend-lease programme because 'they did not really know what they needed' and were unable adequately to co-ordinate the programme. This being

the case, two steps were taken: in response to a request by Chiang Kai-shek that a high ranking air officer be sent to China to survey the needs of the Chinese Air Force, an American-air mission was despatched to China in May 1941. Headed by Brigadier General Henry B Claggett, Commander of the Philippine Air Force, members of the mission visited China from 17th May to 6th June, 1941. The Claggett mission, the first military assistance programme to China sponsored officially by the United States Government, presented its report to the President and the lend-lease administration in July 1941. Its report emphasised China's critical need for fighters and bombers for protection of Chinese cities and to provide a strike force against Japanese bases. Since the Chinese Air Force lacked a sufficient number of adequately trained pilots or facilities for training such pilots, Claggett suggested that Chinese aviation cadets and mechanic trainees be ferried to India or the United States for training. Until such a time as these men could be trained, it was suggested that at least 350 planes (300 fighters, fifty bombers) be immediately despatched to China and manned by American pilots released by the armed services for such purpose. The report, in short, represented a corroboration of the scheme for the creation of an American Volunteer Group originally presented by Chennault in November 1940, a scheme which military leaders had dismissed as insane at the time.

Subsequent to the return of the Claggett mission and the publication of their report, the lend-lease administration approved, in principle, a plan submitted by Lauchlin Currie calling for the eventual release of 500 aircraft to the Chinese to be manned and maintained by Chinese and Americans with the United States providing training for Chinese pilots

**Brigadier-General Henry B Claggett heads the team sent to assess the needs to China's air force**

and mechanics. In addition, it was decided to send a permanent military mission to China to plan and co-ordinate the lend-lease programme. All recommendations were, of course, subject to change, depending upon events in Europe.

Although an American military mission was despatched to China in September 1941, the planes promised to the Chinese Air Force were not received before the Japanese attack on Pearl Harbor (7th December 1941) nor for several months thereafter. Therefore, the American Volunteer Group continued to be China's only effective defence against Japanese air attacks.

**Pearl Harbor precipitates official US involvement**

The Nakajima Ki-27, codenamed NATE by the Allies, was the backbone of the Japanese army's air force in the opening years of the Chinese war, and the army's equivalent, even though it went into service later, of the navy's A5M. It entered service in the summer of 1938. In common with other prewar Japanese fighters, the Ki-27 was underarmed but superlatively manoeuvrable. The Ki-27b superseded the first model on the production lines in late 1938, and was marked by superior visibility for the pilot and provision of bomb dropping or auxiliary fuel tank gear. The type was replaced in front-line service during the year of 1943. Initially, the Ki-27 had been codenamed ABDUL by the Allies in the Burma and China areas, but the name NATE was adopted from 1943 onwards. *Engine:* Army Type 97 (Nakajima Ha-1a) radial, 710hp at takeoff and 780hp at 9,515 feet. *Armament:* Two Type 89 7.7mm machine guns and four 55lb bombs. *Speed:* 292mph at 11,280 feet. *Climb:* 5 minutes 22 seconds to 16,400 feet. *Range:* 390 miles normal and 1,060 miles maximum. *Weight empty/loaded:* 2,447/3,946lbs. *Span:* 37 feet $1\frac{1}{4}$ inches. *Length:* 24 feet $8\frac{1}{2}$ inches

The Mitsubishi A5M4, codenamed CLAUDE by the Allies, first appeared in 1938, replacing earlier models of the ASM, which had first flown in the early months of 1935, and was the Japanese navy's first fighter monoplane. It was finally replaced in first line service in 1942. It was too lightly armed to meet Allied fighters in 1941 and 1942, but its extreme manoeuvrability often enabled it to escape if this became unavoidable. *Engine:* Nakajima Kotobuki 41 or 41 KAI radial, 710hp at take off and 785hp at 9,845 feet. *Armament:* Two Type 89 7.7mm machine guns, plus two 66lb bombs (or one 35-gallon drop tank). *Speed:* 270mph at 9,845 feet. *Climb:* 3 minutes 35 seconds to 9,845 feet. *Ceiling:* 32,150 feet. *Range:* 648 miles with auxiliary tank. *Weight empty/loaded:* 2,681/3,684lbs. *Span:* 36 feet $1\frac{1}{4}$ inches. *Length:* 24 feet $9\frac{3}{4}$ inches. The A5M2b had been provided with an enclosed cockpit, but this had not found favour with Japanese pilots and had therefore been discarded on later models

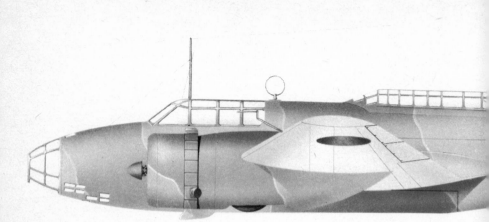

The Japanese army received its first world standard heavy bomber in the late summer of 1938, when the first Mitsubishi Ki-21s were handed over. The type was soon in service in the Chinese theatre, where it had considerable success until the arrival of more formidable fighter opposition than the Chinese could themselves muster. Illustrated in the Ki-21-1a, codenamed JANE by the Allies after the beginning of the Pacific war. *Engines:* Two Army Type 97 (Nakajima Ha-5 KAI) radials, 950hp at takeoff and 1,080hp at 13,125 feet each. *Armament:* Three Type 89 7.7mm machine guns and a bomb load of 1,653lbs normally and 2,205lbs at maximum. *Speed:* 268mph at 13,125 feet. *Climb:* 13 minutes 55 seconds to 13,125 feet. *Ceiling:* 28,215 feet. *Range:* 932 miles normal and 1,680 miles maximum. *Weight empty/loaded:* 10,342/17,452lbs. *Span:* 73 feet 9¾ inches. *Length:* 52 feet 6 inches. *Crew:* 4 to 6. It is worth noting that what the Japanese army called a heavy bomber would have been regarded as only a light to medium bomber by the air forces of the Western Powers

The Nakajima Ki-43 Hayabusa (Peregrine Falcon), codenamed OSCAR was the Japanese Army Air Force's most important fighter in the Second World War. Production was initiated in March 1941. As with other Japanese fighters, the Ki-43 was underarmed and lacking in pilot and fuel protection initially, but aircraft with improvements to overcome this were not used in the China theatre. The type did have, however, the so-called 'butterfly' combat flaps which were featured on several later Japanese fighters. These decreased the aircraft's turning radius, and so made it far more dangerous in a dog fight. In the early months of the Second World War, there were no Allied types that could take on the Hayabusa on equal terms, despite the Japanese fighter's poor armament. The Ki-43's codename had originally been JIM as it was thought that it was a derivative of the NATE with a retractable undercarriage, but later OSCAR was adopted in all the theatres in which the Allies were operating. *Engine:* Army Type 99 (Nakajima Ha-25) radial, 980hp at takeoff and 970hp at 11,155 feet. *Armament:* Two Type 89 7.7mm machine guns or one Type 89 7.7mm and one Type 1 (Ho-103) 12.7mm machine gun, plus two 33-lb bombs. *Speed:* 308mph at 13,125 feet. *Climb:* 5 minutes 30 seconds to 16,400 feet. *Ceiling:* 38,500 feet. *Range:* 745 miles maximum. *Weight empty/loaded:* 3,483/5,695lbs. *Span:* 37 feet $6\frac{1}{4}$ inches. *Length:* 28 feet $11\frac{3}{4}$ inches.

# Battle for Burma

The Japanese attack on Pearl Harbor shattered the illusion of neutrality which had characterised the diplomatic situation between the United Kingdom, the United States, and Japan before 7th December 1941. It would now be only a matter of time until Japanese troops and aircraft would cross the Burma border and preparations were hastily made to combat the Japanese thrust. General Wavell, commander of British forces in Burma, believed he could defend the colony with a minimum of outside aid. He asked only that the Chinese commit one and a half divisions to the defence of Burma and that lend-lease stockpiles destined for China be used by the British in the defence of Burma, should that prove necessary. In ad-

dition, he asked that the AVG contribute one air squadron to the defence of Rangoon. Such was the extent of preparation against the Japanese attack.

On 10th December 1941, a squadron of the American Volunteer Group was moved from the Kyedaw aerodrome to Mingaladon field outside of Rangoon. Consisting of twenty-one planes and twenty-five pilots, the AVG squadron joined a small RAF unit in the defence of Rangoon, the major port of entry and distribution centre of lend-lease goods bound for China. Despite Chennault's reluctance to commit any part of his force to action before the whole group had completed its training, he acceded to Chiang Kai-shek's request that AVG resources be made available

tions in China to Burma, this would be done. Indeed, without the flow of supplies over the Burma Road to China, the likelihood that the AVG could continue to function effectively in China was nil.

The defence of Burma began in Rangoon. Thus, the diversion of one AVG squadron to Mingladon was understandable despite the fact that the twenty-one planes sent there under the command of Arivs Olson represented almost half the operational craft available to Chennault. In fact, of the hundred P-40s purchased for the AVG in January 1941, only fifty-five were airworthy and ready for battle in December 1941. The remaining thirty-four operational planes were evacuated to Kunming on the same day (10th December 1941) that Olson's squadron units moved to Rangoon and the Kyedaw training centre was abandoned. With the arrival of the AVG squadron at Mingaladon aerodrome, the total air garrison at Rangoon numbered only fifty-seven planes, thirty-six of which were antiquated British planes, totally unsuitable for combat against modern Japanese fighters. With no adequate air warning system, this force could hardly be expected to effectively prevent Japanese air raids from devastating the city. That they were able to resist the Japanese at all was a minor miracle.

On 23rd December 1941, the Japanese launched their first raid on Rangoon. Expecting no resistance over the city, the Japanese raiding force retreated quickly after the first exchange with the combined RAF-AVG force. Nevertheless, the raid was costly to the Anglo-American forces. Although they managed to put down at least ten Japanese planes (six bombers and four pursuit craft), the loss of nine planes (four AVG fighters and five RAF planes) was a major disaster for the defenders of Rangoon.

for the defence of Burma.

For the Chinese, even more than for the British, the defence of Burma was absolutely vital. The closing of the Haiphong-Yunnan railroad which followed soon after the Japanese occupation of Indochina in 1940-1941 left the Burma Road as China's only link with the outside world. The Burma Road, which wound its way some 750 miles from Lashio in Burma to Kunming in China, was literally China's lifeline. If the Japanese succeeded in occupying Burma and closing the road, China's ability to resist Japan would be greatly diminished. Therefore, above all else, it was imperative that the Burma Road be protected. If this meant that AVG planes and pilots would have to be diverted from opera-

47

**General Wavell, in command of British forces in Burma, which were inadequately prepared for the Japanese assault**

But more important, perhaps, than the loss of nine planes during the raid, was the effect of the bombing on the people of Rangoon. The results of the bombing attack were devastating. Fires raged throughout the city, thousands were killed or wounded, and many shorefront warehouses were damaged or destroyed. Although British volunteers cleaned up efficiently and attended to the needs of the injured and wounded, they were powerless to prevent the exodus of Burmese and Indian coolies to the countryside. By Christmas 1941, all activities in the city had ground to a halt, resulting in shortages of fuels and other essentials. To prevent looting and rioting, martial law was imposed.

The Japanese returned to Rangoon on 25th December for a second attack. Their strike force, composed of sixty bombers and twenty fighter escorts, broke into two formations just before it reached the city, one heading for the Mingaladon air base and the other for the dock area. This time the Japanese were met by thirteen planes of the AVG. Having been warned of this attack before the Japanese planes reached Rangoon from their bases in Thailand, the AVG were waiting for the Japanese as they flew over Rangoon. For the first time the tactics they had been taught by Chennault at the Kyedaw bases were tested in battle. The result was impressive.

Attacking Japanese formations and diving to attack stray bombers and fighters, the American Volunteer Group routed the Japanese who lost at least twenty-three planes at the hands of the AVG while RAF pilots shot down an additional twelve planes. AVG losses amounted to two of thirteen planes. Clearly, this engagement proved that the unorthodox practices of AVG pilots confused Japanese pilots sufficiently to allow their adversaries an advantage that numbers alone could not provide. After the attack, Radio Tokyo warned the AVG pilots at Rangoon that if they did not abandon their unorthodox tactics they would be 'treated as guerrillas and shown no mercy whatsoever'.

In spite of the fact that they repulsed the Japanese, the men of the combined RAF-AVG garrison had only won a Phyrric victory. Though finally repulsed, some of the Japanese bombers had managed to penetrate the air defence over Rangoon to unload their cargos of bombs. Vital functions in the city were once again brought to a halt and thousands more fled to the countryside hoping to escape from future attacks.

On 28th December, the Japanese sent a small force (fifteen planes) towards Rangoon, but they retreated quickly after first contact with an AVG force of ten P-40s. The AVG planes followed the Japanese through south Burma until forced to land for refuelling. As the fighters were being refuelled, a second Japanese force of thirty planes (ten bombers and twenty pursuits) attacked. With only four planes ready for combat against the Japanese, the result was disastrous. Although joined by twelve RAF planes

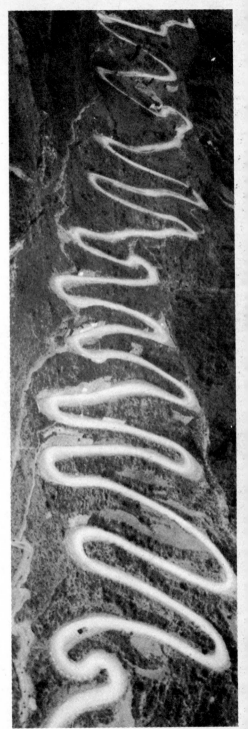

**China's ability to resist comes to depend on the Burma Road—its defence is an AVG priority**

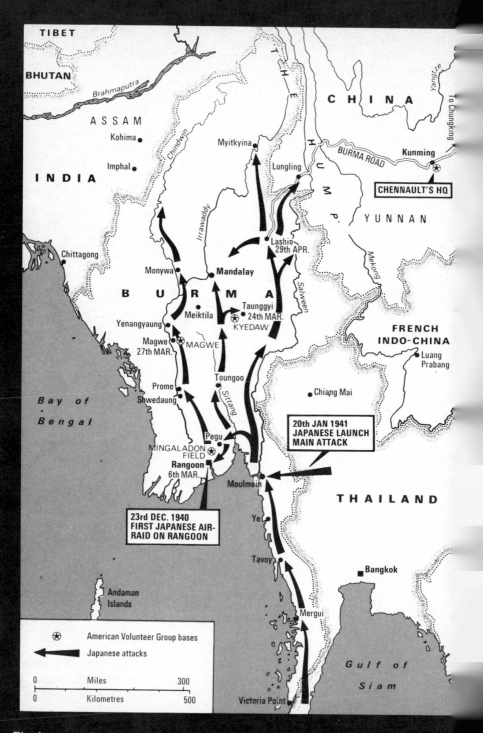

The Japanese invasion of Burma, January/May 1941

forty miles south-east of Rangoon, they were unable to stop the Japanese attack. Ten Japanese bombers reached the Mingaladon aerodrome where they did much damage. Anti-aircraft facilities at the base were antiquated and useless against Japanese planes which flew over the base at an altitude of over 3,000 feet, well beyond the range of the guns. Damage to hangers, fuel storage tanks, and grounded planes was heavy.

The following day, 29th December 1941, the Japanese returned to Rangoon once again, this time concentrating their attack on the city instead of the aerodrome. The raid was more devastating than any to that date. The main railway station was knocked out and wharfs and warehouses filled with lend-lease equipment bound for China were destroyed. Thousands more Burmese and Indians left the city, which was quickly becoming depopulated. Another attack on 31st December completed the city's destruction.

The air raids over Rangoon continued in January 1942 and night raids were launched against the torn city for the first time. The AVG could offer no defence against these raids since their planes were not equipped for night flying. Although they knew the pattern of Japanese attacks, AVG pilots could do nothing to resist and protect the city and the Japanese were thus able to bomb Rangoon almost at will.

But as a result of the night attacks on Rangoon AVG tactics were changed. For the first time in the war, AVG planes struck Japanese air bases in Thailand on 3rd January 1942, establishing a pattern of offensive action to be repeated throughout January and February 1942. Such raids were limited, however, because of shortages of fuel and supplies and the limited range of the P-40s. Because they lacked medium or long range bombers, AVG raids proved to be more of a nuisance to the Japanese than a serious threat and in no way hampered the Japanese advance into Burma.

On 20th January 1942, after almost a month of bombing raids against Rangoon and other military installations in Burma, Japanese land forces crossed the Thai border into southern Burma. Their purpose was to cut the link between Rangoon and Kunming and then to hold Burma as the south-western anchor of a great defensive perimeter stretching from mainland South-East Asia to the south-eastern Pacific.

Moving straight across south Burma, the Japanese easily defeated British, Burmese, and Indian troops defending the approaches to Rangoon. On 23rd February 1942, the Japanese succeeded in ambushing Indian infantry brigades near the Sittang Bridge, crossed the Sittang River, moved past Pegu, and turned south heading toward Rangoon.

With the Japanese victory in the Battle of the Sittang Bridge, the threat to Rangoon became serious. AMMISCA personnel prepared to move lend-lease supplies northwards or destroy them at the docks and warehouses to prevent them falling into Japanese hands. As the Japanese advanced toward Rangoon, lend-lease goods were moved out of the city at a rate of 1,000 tons per day, but even at this accelerated rate of shipment there was not enough time to move all lend-lease stocks in Rangoon north to China. Therefore, much of the equipment in the port was given to the British defence force or destroyed. Nevertheless, when the Japanese captured Rangoon on 6th March 1942, they found 19,052 tons of lend-lease supplies intact in warehouses, including heavy industrial machines, construction equipment and electrical supplies. Before evacuating the city, however, the British destroyed hundreds of guns, millions of rounds of ammunition, and hundreds of trucks and jeeps.

The fury and rapidity of the Japanese advance into Burma far exceeded

anything that the defenders of Burma had anticipated. As the Japanese drew near to Rangoon, Wavell hastily requested additional Chinese aid, aid that had been offered to him at the beginning of February 1942 but refused. Despite the ill-will between Chiang and Wavell – resulting from Wavell's original failure to consult the Generalissimo when preparing for the defence of Burma – Chiang responded to Wavell's request for aid and Chinese forces began to move across the Sino-Burmese border on 28th February 1942.

Shortly after the Japanese captured Rangoon (6th March 1942), Chinese forces were massed in Toungoo and points to the north of that city while British and Indian units were concentrated in Mandalay, Prome, and Yenangyaung. It was Wavell's intention to hold these centres against the Japanese and cut the road from Rangoon to Mandalay. If the Japanese could be held south of Prome and Toungoo, the oil fields at Yenang-yaung, China's major source of crude oil, would be protected and the completion of a new road from Assam to Burma, linking the Indian ports of Calcutta and Chittagong to Kuomin-tang held Yunnan province, would be facilitated. Over such a new road, lend-lease supplies could once again be funnelled into China.

After taking Rangoon, Japanese units moved northwards along the Sittang and Irrawaddy rivers toward Prome and Toungoo. As they moved, they were harrassed by RAF and AVG pilots flying out of their new base at Magwe, 200 miles north of Rangoon. In an effort to destroy Magwe, the Japa-

**British flags still fly at a frontier railway bridge as the arrival of the Japanese vanguard heralds the invasion of Burma**

**Japanese G3M2 'Nell' bombers en route for their target**

nese launched a series of massive bombing raids against the base from 21st to 27th March 1942, using all available bombers at their disposal in Burma (200) for this purpose. The Japanese raids against Magwe forced the rapid abandonment and evacuation of the base; with its loss and the retreat of the RAF into India and the AVG into China, Allied air strength in Burma was almost completely destroyed, leaving the Japanese in control of the skies over southern Burma.

The loss of air cover and the absence of adequate aerial reconnaissance after the destruction of the Magwe aerodrome left the British and Chinese easy prey for the Japanese who had secured detailed information about Allied troop displacements and movements from Burmese nationalist groups. Thus, when the Japanese moved toward Prome and Toungoo, they quickly took the cities inflicting heavy losses on the retreating defenders of Burma.

**The heartbreaking but necessary scorched earth policy; valuable machinery and stores are destroyed to prevent their capture by the enemy**

The Japanese began their attack on Toungoo on 19th March 1942, capturing the Kyedaw aerodrome, the original training base of the AVG, on 24th March. As the Japanese prepared to march north from Toungoo, General Joseph Stilwell, American Military Commander in the CBI theatre and Wavell's lieutenant in the defence of Burma, sought to persuade Chinese commanders to counterattack the Japanese in Toungoo and retake the airfield at Kyedaw. Failing in this, he persuaded the British commanders in the area to launch the attack. Their attack was feeble and disastrous. British units were routed at Shwedaung and, forced to abandon their armoured vehicles, fleeing from the area on foot on 29th March, a day after the counterattack had been launched. The failure of the Allies to retake Kyedaw left the AVG-RAF

units with one less base from which to launch attacks on Japanese forces.

Japanese victories at Toungoo and Prome emasculated the Allied plan to cut the Rangoon-Mandalay road. Moreover, as the Japanese advanced northwards from these cities, capturing Magwe, Meiktila, and Taunggyi in rapid succession, Yemangyaung, Mandalay, and Lashio were threatened. As a Japanese victory in Burma became an increasing reality, steps were taken to evacuate these important centres. The British prepared to destroy all stores and supplies which might be of use to the Japanese, including the oil fields and depots at Yenangyaung. At the same time, airfields in central and northern Burma was evacuated and AVG operations from Burmese bases were brought to an end.

Lashio, the southern terminus of the Burma Road, fell to the Japanese on 29th April, along with 44,000 tons of lend-lease supplies destined for China. With the closing of the Burma Road, the only land routes to China were the old silk highway across the Sinkiang province from Russia and the caravan trails across the Himalayas and through Tibet from India. Neither of these routes were ideal for transporting large quantities of goods and supplies to China. To reach the borders of Sinkiang, American and British supplies would have to be moved through crowded Russian ports and then thousands of miles over overburdened and inadequate Russian railways. After this goods would have to be transferred to trucks and pack animals for the slow journey to the war front in China. The caravan trails through Tibet offered a much shorter route but only pack animals could negotiate the mountain trails. The trip was slow, and heavy equipment could not be carried. Thus, the fall of Lashio represented a crushing blow to the Chinese, one from which they might never have recovered had it not been for the establishment of an air lift over the 'Hump'. The loss of the Burma Road was a serious blow to the Allied cause.

With the fall of Lashio, Allied forces retreated rapidly toward China. During the retreat, the American Volunteer group played an important role in three ways. Firstly, AVG planes, flying from bases in China, provided the only source of reconnaissance and Intelligence available to the Allies. Secondly, AVG pilots provided air cover to the retreating Chinese armies. Thirdly, AVG pilots destroyed the northern portion of the Burma Road and bridges across the Salween River, thus preventing – or at least inhibiting – a Japanese advance from Burma into Yunnan.

AVG reconnaissance missions were inaugurated in March 1942 and the majority of AVG missions after the fall of Toungoo (24th March) and Magwe (27th March) were patrol and reconnaissance missions. In part, the switch from combat to patrol missions was dictated by shortages of equipment and fuel. Although AVG pilots disliked such missions and considered them to be dangerous and a waste of precious resources, with fewer than forty planes serviceable following the evacuation of all AVG bases in Burma in April 1942, the AVG could hardly sustain a regular programme of defensive strikes. Moreover, since the AVG had no bombers at its disposal, offensive raids against Japanese bases in Thailand or occupied Chinese were of limited value and could hardly blunt the Japanese advance in Burma. Thus, in the lull between battle action, AVG pilots were assigned to reconnaissance patrols during March and April 1942. However, as the retreat of Allied forces towards the Chinese border moved into full swing in May the AVG once again resumed combat activities.

The evacuation of Allied forces to China necessitated the destruction of bases and supplies in Burma. In addition, in order to prevent the Japanese from crossing the Salween into China, bridges and other installations leading to the river had to be destroyed while, at the same time, strafing and bombing raids were flown against Japanese troop movements to slow their rapid advance. To accomplish these tasks, optimum use had to be made of the limited number of planes still serviceable.

To maximise the use of available aircraft and minimise equipment losses, AVG units were scattered over several bases in China. Strikes against the Japanese were launched from various bases and planes were never immediately returned to the same base from which they had taken off. This accomplished two things. The Japanese were kept off balance by the total mobility of the AVG units and, more importantly, overestimated the numbers of planes available to their enemies. Had the Japanese realised the real strength of the AVG, they would have been encouraged to take even bolder steps in the Burma campaign.

Attempts to procure additional planes for the American Volunteer

The standard fighter used by the American Volunteer Group in China was the
Curtiss Hawk 81A-3. These were originally a group of 100 P-40Cs for Great Britain,
but as they were not of a sufficiently high performance to take on German fighters
over Western Europe, they were transferred to the Chinese air force, who in turn
forwarded them to the AVG in the southern China/Burma area. These went into
action for the first time during December 1941. Though possessing the sturdiness
and pleasant flight characteristics of all American fighters, they were outclassed by
the more modern of the fighters employed by the Japanese against the Chinese
except in their strength, armour protection and diving performance, the last
enabling many American pilots to escape from tricky situations in which they would
otherwise have perished. Against the older Japanese fighters and the bombers they
had more success. Nevertheless, the success of the AVG should be credited to the
great skill and energy of its pilots rather than the performance of its aircraft.
*Engine:* Allison V-1710-33 inline, 1,040hp at 15,000 feet. *Armament:* Two .5-inch and
four .3-inch Browning machine guns. *Speed:* 345mph at 15,000 feet. *Climb:* 2,690
feet per minute initially and 5.1 minutes to 15,000 feet. *Ceiling:* 29,500 feet. *Range:*
730 miles normal and 945 miles maximum. *Weight empty/loaded:* 5,812/7,549lbs.
*Span:* 37 feet 3½ inches. *Length:* 31 feet 8½ inches (Plan and side view over page).

Group during the latter part of the Burma campaign were largely futile. Since the AVG was not formally part of the United States armed forces, it had low priority when it came to purchase of supplies and equipment in the United States. Chennault's pleas for the transfer of aircraft and pilots from the Tenth Army Air Force command in India to his command in Kunming were denied for the same reason. Only after the immediacy of the Allied collapse in Burma was established was aid promised and even then little of the promised equipment was received before or immediately after the fall of Burma.

As the Burma campaign drew to a close, AVG morale hit its low point. The cumulative strain of countless combat missions, the lack of adequate equipment and the feeling of isolation led to a crisis in which twenty-four pilots of the American Volunteer

Group offered their resignations to Chennault in late April 1942. A crisis was averted when Chennault persuaded all but four of the men to withdraw their resignations or face charges of desertion. Nevertheless, the bitter experiences of AVG pilots in Burma were not soon forgotten and when the American Volunteer Group was finally incorporated into the Army Air Force in July the same year very few of the original members of the AVG volunteered to continue their careers in China as members of the newly formed China Air Task Force (CATF) commanded by Chennault.

But despite shortages in supplies and equipment, failing morale, and the deteriorating situation of the Allies in Burma, the men of the American Volunteer Group performed as bravely and effectively as circumstances permitted in the last weeks of

**A Japanese soldier observes the Burma Road from a commanding height above the Salween Gorge. Flying Tigers destroyed bridges to slow the Japanese advance**

the Burma campaign. With the Japanese poised to cross the Salween river from Burma into China by 1st May, AVG pilots were ordered to destroy all bridges across the Salween and access roads from Burma to Yunnan. The destruction of these facilities would cost the lives of hundreds if not thousands of civilian refugees fleeing from the Japanese, but Chiang Kaishek had no alternative but to sign the order. On 7th May, Chennault received the following message from Chungking: 'Generalissimo instructs you send all available AVG planes to attack trucks and boats between Salween and Lungling City. Notify AVG that he appreciates their loyalty and redoubled efforts particularly at this juncture. . . .'

The attack ordered by Chiang Kaishek on the Japanese armies advancing toward Yunnan was brutally successful. The rapid advance of Japanese forces northwards through Burma and the collapse of all effective resistance to this advance at the end of April had led many observers to the conclusion that it would not be long before the Japanese would reach Kunming. But the Japanese never crossed the Salween. This fact has been attributed by some to the efficacy of AVG strikes against the vanguard of the Japanese advance, the 56th Division of the Japanese Fifteenth Army. Others, including staff officers of the Fifteenth Army, maintained that there was never any plan to invade Yunnan. Whether or not this was the case, AVG attacks on Japanese units near the Salween were

**Natural cover hides planes from aerial observation while urgent repairs are carried out**

Chennault proudly displays the new
official Flying Tiger emblem

quite successful. Monsoon rains
shielded the Japanese from attack
for much of the month of May,
but following a break in the rains on
25th May, daily raids were launched
against Japanese installations south
of the Salween. All regular links
between Burma and China were temporarily broken and the Japanese
suffered thousands of casualties and
considerable loss of equipment.

In retrospect, the performance of
the American Volunteer Group in the
Burma campaign was impressive.
Between 23rd December 1941 and 1st
July 1942, AVG pilots destroyed at
least 299 Japanese planes and probably
damaged or destroyed another 300
planes. In addition, their strafing
raids against the Japanese cost the
enemy thousands of lives and an unknown loss of equipment. Considering
the resources available to the AVG,
this record was amazing. With no
more than fifty-five planes airworthy
at any given time and only seventy-
nine pilots trained to Chennault's
specifications to fly them, the men of
the AVG performed an amazing task
winning both the affection of the
Chinese who nicknamed them the
'Flying Tigers' and the admiration of
the American people who followed
their escapades with pride at a time
when their's were the only victories in
the war. On the other hand, it is
important to note, as many of the
biographers of Chennault and the
AVG have failed to do, that the AVG
could not and did not prevent the
Japanese from the occupation of
Burma. Given the inadequate preparation for the defence of Burma, it is
doubtful if a force even twice as large
as the original AVG could have
succeeded in preventing the Japanese
victory in Burma. In any event,
dreams of a second and third American Volunteer Group never material-
ised, the American Volunteer Group
could not stop the Japanese alone.

# China Air Task Force

As long as the American Volunteer Group remained independent of the armed forces of the United States, there was little possibility of obtaining additional equipment and personnel. Moreover, since for all practical purposes the AVG functioned as part of the Allied team in Burma after Pearl Harbor and the Japanese invasion of Burma, there was little reason to remain apart from the American command in the China-Burma-India theatre, particularly in view of the fact that as a part of the United States Army Air Force Chennault and his men might expect considerably higher priority in the procurement of equipment and supplies. Thus, when the army offered to reactivate Chennault and incorporate his American Volunteer Unit into the Tenth Army Air Force, Chennault accepted the offer, voluntarily giving up the independence and autonomy he enjoyed as commander of the AVG. Chiâng Kai-shek, under whose command the AVG had functioned as an irregular unit of the Chinese Air Force, also agreed to the chang believing that as a unit of the Arm, Air Force, Chennault's men coul( offer more adequate aerial protection to China.

The idea of incorporating the AVG into the Tenth Army Air Force was first formally presented to Chennault by Lieutenant-General Joseph Stilwell, Commander-in-Chief of the American forces in the CBI theatre, on 4th March 1942. Chennault's acceptance of this proposition came as 'a big relief' to Stilwell, who had feared that Chennault might not wish to work with him or see the AVG merged with the Army Air Forces. According to their original agreement, the AVG would be merged with the Tenth Air Force in April 1942 and in anticipation of this, Chennault was reactivated by the army and promoted to the rank of Brigadier-General and placed in command of the

**Lieutenant-General Joseph Stilwell. He proposed to Chennault the merging of the AVG with Tenth Army Air Force**

Flying Tigers claim a 'flying tiger' of a different breed. This emblem is on the tail fin of a downed Japanese reconnaissance plane

newly organised China Air Task Force (CATF).

In fact, the China Air Task Force was not activated until 4th July 1942, three months after the original agreement to merge the AVG with the Tenth Air Force. This delay was undoubtedly due to the reluctance of the large majority of the members of the American Volunteer Group to accept induction into the Army Air Force before or after the expiration of their contracts with CAMCO on 4th July 1942. Since most members of the American Volunteer Group had indicated their unwillingness to stay on in China if inducted into the Army Air Force, Chennault had no alternative but to postpone the incorporation of the AVG into the Army Air Force until the CAMCO contracts expired and new men and equipment arrived so that there would be no lapse in air cover in China.

Much has been made of the unwillingness of the original Flying Tigers to accept induction into the Army Air Force. Some have laid the blame for this on the fact that the men of the AVG were little more than mercenaries interested in the defence of China only in so far as they netted $500.00 for each Japanese plane downed and continued to draw a high monthly salary from CAMCO. Others prefer to explain the AVG-CATF *débâcle* in terms of the tactless manner in which Army Air Force recruiters went about the process of trying to induct the men of the AVG into the Tenth Air Force. Many explained the lack of enthusiasm for the merger with the Army Air Force in terms of war-weariness and the desire of the men to return home. In ll probability, there is some truth to each of these suggestions. In any case, when the idea of a merger was first suggested to the men of the American Volunteer Group they rejected it almost unanimously. Having joined the AVG to escape the regimentation and red tape of official military service, the men were not anxious to return to it. None of them originally volunteered to accept induction into the Army Air Force and even after Chennault appealed to them personally to stay on in China, only five members of the AVG chose to stay on in China under a new command.

The China Air Task Force was finally activated on 4th July 1942. As a unit of the Tenth Air Force based in India, activities of the CATF were subject to the veto of Tenth Air Force commander, Brigadier-General Clayton Bissell. This situation created two problems, the most serious of which was the problem of communication and coordination. Chennault's headquarters at Kunming was located 2,200 miles away from Tenth Air Force HQ

in Delhi. Because of this distance between headquarters and the difficulty of co-ordinating and supplying the CATF from India, the China Air Task Force continued to operate independently of the command in Delhi. When the idea of a merger of the AVG and the Tenth Air Force was first considered, the problems that would be posed by the separation of commands was recognised by the War Department, but it was nonetheless deemed advisable to proceed with the merger since the United States could not afford to create and sustain an independent Air Force in China at that time. Indeed, at the time the CATF was created, the Tenth Air Force was itself hardly more than a paper command with only eighteen operational aircraft (eight bombers and ten fighters) – fewer planes even than the AVG.

More important than the distance between CATF and Tenth Air Force commands was the lack of cooperation between Chennault and his immediate superior, Bissell. Friction

Major-General Clayton Bissell. As Brigadier-General he commanded Tenth Air Force in July 1942

Mme Chiang Kai-shek. Her close relationship with Chennault did nothing to ease the friction between him and his superiors

between the two men, which long predated their wartime relationship, often reflected fundamental differences over strategy and tactics rather than a mere clash of personalities. Chennault balked at subordinating himself to a man who had consistently criticised his theories of the use of air power in the past. Making matters even worse was the fact that Bissell had been promoted to the rank of Brigadier - General one day before Chennault was promoted to the same rank, thus giving him seniority over Chennault and all the prerogatives that such seniority conferred. Chennault never accepted this situation gracefully and persisted in the belief that the timing of Bissell's promotion represented a conscious attempt of the part of the theatre commander, General Stilwell, to keep him in check. On the other hand, if Chennault distrusted Bissell and Stilwell, they disliked his arrogance and independence of mind. Even more, they feared his close relationship with Generalissimo and Madame Chiang Kai-shek and felt that every time there was some disagreement between them and Chennault, he would appeal over their heads to Chiang, who would send Madame Chiang off to Washington DC to plead Chennault's case at the War Department and the White House. Command problems continued to plague the relationship between the CATF and Tenth Air Force command until March 1943.

Shortly after assuming command of the China Air Task Force, Chennault submitted a memorandum to Stilwell outlining his views on the potential of China-based air power. Chennault's objectives for the CATF were sixfold: 1 to protect the air supply route over the Hump; 2 to destroy Japanese aircraft in China in large numbers; 3 to

**C-46 Commando awaits its turn to take off for the trip across the Hump**

damage and destroy Japanese military and naval bases in China and encourage Chinese resistance; 4 to disrupt Japanese shipping on the Yangtze and Yellow rivers and along the China coast; 5 to damage Japanese bases in Thailand, Indo-China, Burma, and Formosa and interdict Japanese air concentrations being ferried from Chinese bases across Indo-China and Thailand to Burma; 6 to destroy the efficacy and morale of the Japanese Air Force by destroying rear depôts and aircraft production facilities in Japan. To accomplish these objectives, Chennault asked Stilwell for a hundred new P-51 fighters and thirty B-25 bombers and operational independence from Bissell's command in Delhi. A copy of this memorandum was also sent to Chiang Kai-shek.

**The Hump—the Himalayas between India and China**

Stilwell was not opposed to the aggressive spirit of Chennault's memorandum of 16th September However, he urged moderation in view of shortages of equipment and supply and suggested to both Chennault and the Generalissimo that for the time being CATF activities be limited primarily to defending the ferry route from India to China and, secondarily, to conduct operations against Japanese shipping, aircraft, and installations where munitions were available for such operations and when they did not jeopardise the primary function of the AVG – the protection of the Hump airlift. Despite the criticism levelled against Stilwell by Chennault and his supporters, there is no indication that at this time (September 1942) he was opposed to maximising the use of air power in China. On the contrary, whatever limitations he suggested to Chennault and Chiang were based on

the exigencies of supply and not, as Stilwell's detractors have too frequently assumed, on the personal hostility between Stilwell and Chennault.

Chennault's plan, presented to Stilwell and Chiang in his memorandum of 16th September, went well beyond the capabilities of his tiny force, at this time consisting of only forty-seven operational planes and no fuel reserves or stockpiles of spare parts. To bring his ambitions' within the realm of the achievable would have required equipment and supplies which could not be obtained at the time.

Little could be done by Chennault or his immediate superiors to alter the decision of the Joint Chiefs of Staff to defeat the Japanese in the Pacific as opposed to China. On the other hand, the administration of the air ferry from India to China was controlled by Chennault's superiors, Bissell and Stilwell. Since the China Air Task Force was almost totally dependent on the air lift and its success hinged on the ability of the Tenth Air Force to fly in the tonnage necessary for their combat operations, the airlift quickly became a bone of contention between Delhi and Kunming.

Chennault never accepted the fact that the air ferry operation was insufficient to provide him with the supplies necessary to permit him to carry out his air plan. Since the only restraint on the operations of Chennault's units was the inability of the Hump to furnish adequate supplies, he scrutinised the air lift thoroughly and came to the conclusion that it could sustain his programme if priorities were correctly arranged. But Stilwell decided the priorities for the Hump lift, Chennault accused Stilwell of failing to give the matter sufficient

**Line-up of P-40Ks**

consideration and the relationship between the two men rapidly worsened.

Stilwell apparently made little effort to cultivate a good relationship with his air commander in China, but records indicate that he did not purposely go out of his way to obstruct the flow of supplies to the China Air Task Force. Factors beyond his control hampered the passage of supplies to the CATF. There was a shortage of cargo planes to fly the air ferry route and the flight over the Himalayas was difficult and dangerous. In addition, monsoon rains and winds frequently caused the cancellation of Hump flights for days at a time. And even when planes made their regular flights from India to China, there was considerable difficulty in moving goods from Kunming to the forward bases of the CATF which were located

in regions surrounded by the Japanese and defended by poorly equipped and supplied Chinese armies. Under such circumstances it would normally not have been feasible to continue supply operations to these bases. However, because of promises made to Chiang Kai-shek that Chennault's operations would be maintained where possible, the movement of supplies to these bases continued.

Chennault understood the risks involved in flying the Hump and the difficulties of moving supplies from Kunming to the hinterland, but he continued to believe that within the capacity of the airlift to move supplies to China there should be a more judicious use of available space for transport of war needs and it was for this reason that he was most critical of Stilwell. He was particularly angered at the amount of precious lift tonnage devoted to useless office supplies and other such non-essen-

**Republic P-43s**

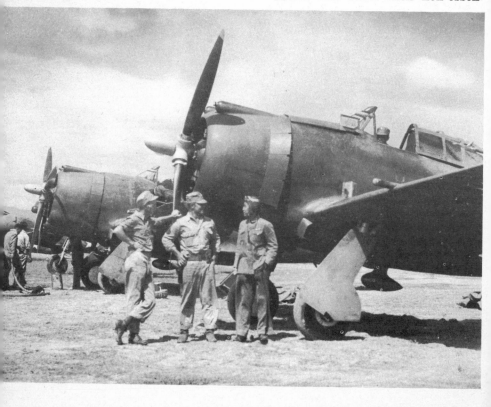

**B-25 Mitchell**

tials. While this criticism was not invalid, what Chennault often failed to realise was that much of this material was bound for the headquarters of the Chinese Nationalist Government in Chungking and had been requisitioned by the Generalissimo and not by Stilwell, who was himself critical of the fact that so much valuable space on the cargo planes was given to the carrying of non-essentials. According to statistics compiled by Stilwell's staff, in the six months ending in February 1943, nine per cent of all tonnage flown over the Hump (837 tons) was Chinese paper money, engraved in Brooklyn, New York and flown to China. Considering the risks involved in the air ferry operation, from the military point of view, such cargoes were a luxury that the CBI theatre could not afford but could do little about. Chiang Kai-shek was as much to blame as were Stilwell and Bissell.

Given the shortage of supplies and equipment in China and the inability of the air ferry supply route to support a widely expanded air war in China, the operations of the China Air Task Force, like those of the American Volunteer Group before it, deviated from standard Army Air Force procedures. The CATF continued to operate as 'air guerrillas' after the fashion of the original AVG.

But the activation of the China Air Task Force did not result in any immediate improvement in the material situation of what had been the American Volunteer Group. In fact, the situation of American air power in China worsened due to the loss of the majority of the experienced pilots of the AVG. The CATF inherited fifty-seven planes (fifty-four P-40s, three P-43s) from the AVG of which only forty were operable and eight bombers (B-25s) from the Tenth Air Force of which only seven were airworthy. There were few spare parts for these planes and little high octane gasoline

**Airfields in China must be constructed very much by hand if other means are not available**

to fly them. With a total force of forty-seven operational aircraft, the CATF faced an enemy with capabilities vastly exceeding its own along a 2,000 mile frontier stretching from Honkew to Hong Kong and Burma to Indo-China.

The primary mission of the China Air Task Force was to defend the southern and eastern approaches to the Hump and its China terminals. The CATF's secondary mission was to attack and harass Japanese shipping and supply. Thirdly, the CATF was to provide air support for Chinese armies in Yunnan and east China. To accomplish these missions with the meagre resources available necessitated

maximum utilisation of equipment and personnel and the development of an efficient air warning network, both of which were accomplished by Chennault.

As preparations were made for the transition of the American Volunteer Group to the China Air Task Force, Chennault worked out a scheme to maximise the offensive capabilities of the CATF while providing adequate protection for the air ferry over the Hump. The key to this plan was mobility and the distribution of available aircraft over several bases. To support this kind of operation tens of thousands of Chinese coolies laboured to construct a series of airfields in arcs stretching from Chungto and Chung-king to the north-west and north, Hengyang, Ling-ling, and Kweilin or the east, Nanning to the south-east

and Kunming and Yunnani to the south and west. From these bases, the men of the CATF were able to protect the Hump and strike against Japanese installations in China, Indo-China, Thailand and Burma.

In the months after the activation of the China Air Task Force, the CATF pilots mastered the art of hit and run attacks on the Japanese from their string of bases on the perimeter of Japanese controlled China. Extreme mobility became the hallmark of CATF action in which the optimum use was made of limited equipment. This strategy was designed to keep the Japanese off balance and their Intelligence men guessing.

To keep the Japanese from acquiring exact knowledge of the number of planes available to the China Air Task Force, several devices were used including painting spinners on the propellers

**A Liberator passes above a Chinese work party levelling a runway with a massive stone roller**

different colours, changing numbers on the fuselages, and rotating attacks from different bases. The result was that the Japanese believed that the China Air Task Force was far larger than it actually was and were reluctant to initiate major actions against the CATF. In the autumn of 1942, Japanese estimates placed the strength of the CATF at 200 planes. Actually, at the time, there were only forty-seven operatiọnal planes available to the CATF but the serial number of these planes had been reversed so many times that the Japanese could not estimate the true number of CATF planes.

Chennault's rotation of men and equipment, which frequently left bases undefended or partially defended, could hardly have been successful had it not been for the somewhat crude, though extraordinarily efficient air warning system operating at CATF facilities. Warning networks were established around each aerodrome in concentric circles of 100 and 200 kilometres from the centre of the fields. Within these circles, there were thousands of reporting stations, some deep within enemy lines. Chinese volunteers (interceptors) manned these stations and relayed information from behind Japanese lines to stations nearer to the aerodrome, from which point they were relayed to Intelligence headquarters at the various bases. Interceptors were trained to recognise and distinguish between various kinds of Japanese aircraft and they relayed Japanese activities to central headquarters via radio transmitters smuggled in from Hong Kong and assembled in Yunnan. Thus, when the Japanese launched raids against CATF bases, before the planes got to within fifty minutes flying time from the American airfields, the men of the CATF knew what kinds and number of planes were flying against them and in what direction they were coming. Rarely did the Japanese launch an attack which was not known in advance by the CATF.

The value of this Intelligence network was incalculable. Because Chennault always knew where the Japanese were going and what they were flying, he was able to use his meagre resources successfully against great odds, thus enabling his small force of less than a hundred planes to operate for several months against an enemy which could muster at least 500 aircraft. The air warning network also served to guide lost CATF pilots back to base, saving valuable equipment and lives in the process.

Although the China Air Task Force

Tengchung is bombed by B-25s of Chennault's command

**Kweilin airfield, constructed to make best use of natural features, is base for attacks on Japanese shipping in Hong Kong harbour**

was not formally activated until 4th July 1942, it was baptised on 3rd July in a pre-emptive raid against Japanese Air Force installations in occupied China. This raid was based on Intelligence reports of a major strike against AVG installations planned by the Japanese for 4th July to wipe out the CATF at the very outset of its existence. The Japanese believed that the dissolution of the American Volunteer Group on 4th July – a fact known to Japanese Intelligence units for several weeks before the 4th – would mean an end to the air guerilla tactics so successfully used against them in the past. Since the Japanese also knew that few AVG pilots had volunteered to serve in the China Air Task Force after the expiration of their contracts with CAMCO, they believed that by striking against the inexperienced new pilots of the CATF before they were introduced to the Chennault tactical training programme, they might destroy the CATF on the ground with one massive blow. They did not know, however, that Chennault was aware of their plans and that he had persuaded twenty AVG pilots to stay on in China until the CATF could be brought up to full strength and new pilots instructed in the methods of the AVG.

During the first weeks after the activation of the China Air Task Force, contact with the Japanese was frequent and a pattern of action was established which was followed for the next six months. With the arrival of eight B-25s from India, Chennault for the first time had limited offensive capacity and was able to hit Japanese targets hitherto immune from the basically defensive tactics of the American Volunteer Group. During the fortnight after 4th July 1942, bombers of the CATF ran four offensives against Japanese installations

in or near Canton, Hankow, and Tengchung. The B-25s were accompanied on these raids by P-40 fighter escorts, some of which were equipped to carry additional bombs. After the bombers deposited their loads, fighters strafed enemy installations, often causing more damage than the bombers themselves. At the cost of five P-40s and one B-25, pilots of the China Air Task Force destroyed twenty-four Japanese fighters and twelve bombers.

In August 1942, CATF pilots continued their offensive against the Japanese. CATF fighters strafed Japanese bases at Lingchuan, Yochow, Nanchang, and Sienning, while the bombers were sent over Burma and Indo-China, doing considerable damage to warehouses and wharfs in Haiphong and Japanese military installations at Myitkyina and Lashio. After the first two weeks of the month these raids ended due to a shortage of aviation fuel and the need to repair aircraft. They were resumed on 26th August.

In September, eastern China once again became the centre of CATF activities. Fighters strafed Japanese bases south of the Yangtze while the B-25s continued to attack Hankow and the Hanoi-Haiphong area. In October, India based B-24 bombers were temporarily deployed in China and with the B-25s of the CATF launched the first American raids against major Japanese targets north of the Yellow River.

On 25th October, the men of the China Air Task Force executed a daring attack on Japanese shipping in Hong Kong harbour. Flying from Kweilin and undetected by the Japanese until reaching Hong Kong, twelve B-25s accompanied by seven P-40s dropped 30,000 pounds of demolition and 1,700 pounds of fragmentation bombs. This attack was followed by a night raid that evening, the first ever flown by the CATF. Six unescorted B-25s successfully completed their mission to knock out power plants in Hong Kong with no losses. Total losses for the entire operation, both

**A native helper loads fuel for transport over the Hump**

day and evening, were two planes (one B-25 and one P-40), whereas the Japanese lost twenty-one interceptors in the engagement. Once again Chennault proved what could be done with proper use of air power.

Offensive actions against Japanese installations in Burma, China, and Indo-China were continued in December 1942 but as the new year approached shortages of fuel and spare parts forced the curtailment of all CATF activities. With the closing of the Burma Road, all aviation gasoline had to be flown over the Hump. To reach the forward bases of the CATF in east China, the gasoline had to be carried or rolled by Chinese coolies over hundreds of miles of dirt roads. To carry one day's supply of fuel from Kunming to Kweilin took forty days if the drums of gasoline were carried by cart and seventy-five days if rolled by coolies. One day's action by a fighter group or one bomber might deplete several week's worth of supply effort. Thus, for the men of the CATF every drop of gasoline was valuable.

During the first months of 1943 the supply problem became so acute that the China Air Task Force lacked sufficient fuel to engage in any offensive missions. Therefore, only when the Japanese had crossed the inner circles of the air warning systems (within a hundred kilometres of a given CATF installation) could planes be sent up to protect these bases. As might be expected, Chennault could not accept this situation. Blaming the shortages of fuel and supplies on Bissell or Stilwell, he pressed on with his plan to separate the CATF from the Tenth Air Force and create an air force in China independent of the Delhi command. Given the impressive record of the China Air Task Force in 1942, he found considerable enthusiasm for his scheme in Chungking and Washington.

# Chennault versus Stilwell

From the outset of his career in China, Chennault persisted in the belief that the war in China should be primarily an air war. Thus, when it became clear to him that as long as the American Volunteer Group operated independently of the Army Air Force it would be doomed to fighting the Japanese with poor equipment and almost no supplies, he agreed to dissolve the group and assume command of the China Air Task Force. Unfortunately for Chennault, when the AVG was incorporated into the Tenth Army Air Force, its material situation did not change perceptively. There was still no new equipment and, even more important, he and his superior, General Stilwell, failed to agree upon the role and importance of air power in the CBI Theatre.

The increasing success of CATF operations reaffirmed Chennault's belief that the key to winning the war against Japan at the least cost lay in the imaginative use of air power. Given some additional aircraft and *carte blanche* to deploy them from

bases in China, Chennault projected that he could destroy the enemy efficiently and quickly. All Japanese installations were readily accessible from CATF bases in China and new bases would extend the capabilities of the CATF. By jabbing at the Japanese and gradually reducing their capacity to move equipment and supplies, the American advance in the Pacific would be facilitated. If the Japanese were to meet this aerial offensive against them in China, they would have to divert forces from elsewhere which might weaken them. Thus, as far as Chennault was concerned investment in men and aircraft could not fail to pay off.

The substance of Chennault's views on the use of air power in China was conveyed to General Stilwell in a series of memoranda in the autumn of 1942. At that time, as mentioned in the last chapter, Stilwell responded less than enthusiastically to Chennault's proposals. Although he commended Chennault for his aggressive spirit, he vetoed any extensive aerial

programme in China. Moreover, he rejected Chennault's proposal to separate the CATF from the Tenth Air Force command in Delhi.

But Chennault never accepted the validity of Stilwell's reservations about the potential of air power in China and lost no opportunity to criticise Stilwell's military judgement and push his own plan, which had already been enthusiastically received by Chiang Kai-shek and his Chungking clique. Thus, when Wendell Wilkie, unsuccessful Republican candidate for the Presidency of the United States in 1940, visited China in October 1942 as President Roosevelt's special emissary, Chennault outlined his strategy to him in a meeting at Chennault's office on 8th October 1942. While Stilwell sat in the outer office waiting, Chennault and Wilkie discussed the war in China.

Wilkie was amazed to find out that Chennault was operating with less than ten bombers and fifty fighters. Like many others who had followed the activities of the China Air Task

**Wendell L Wilkie, convert to Chennault's ideas, takes leave of Mme and Generalissimo Chiang Kai-shek in Chungking**

Force in the press, Wilkie had assumed that the range of such activities dictated that the CATF force numbered many more planes than Chennault actually had at his disposal. Concerned that Wilkie's reaction might be shared by the President and others in Washington, Chennault asked Wilkie to carry a letter from him to Roosevelt. Wilkie, having been successfully converted by Chennault, agreed and returned to Washington with Chennault's letter.

In his letter to Roosevelt, dated 8th October 1942, Chennault expressed the view that Japan could be defeated by effective use of air power and requested authority to build and command an enlarged and independent air force in China. He stated that if he was supplied with 105 fighters, thirty medium bombers, twelve heavy bombers, and sufficient stores of spare parts he could bring about 'the downfall of Japan', saving the lives of hundreds of thousands of American sailors and soldiers in the process.

To accomplish this he deemed it essential to be given complete freedom of action and direct access to Chiang Kai-shek and the Chinese government. The military task of defeating Japan was, according to Chennault, a simple one which had been complicated by unwieldly, illogical military organisations and by men who did not understand aerial warfare and its potential.

Chennault summed up his plan to Roosevelt in the following manner: 'Japan must hold Hong Kong, Shanghai, and the Yangtze valley. They are essential to hold Japan itself. I can force the Japanese Air Force to fight in the defence of these objectives

**General George C Marshall. He had reservations about Chennault's plans for increased scope and independence**

believed the best air warning net of its kind in the world. With the use of these tactics, I am confident that I can destroy Japanese aircraft at the rate of between ten and twenty, to one. When the Japanese Air Force refuses to come within my warning net and fight, I will strike out with my medium bombers against the sea supply line to the Southwest Pacific. In a few months the enemy will lose so many aircraft that the aerial defence of Japan will be negligible. I can then strike Japan with heavy bombers. My air force can burn up Japan's two main industrial areas, Tokyo and the Kobe-Osaka-Nagoya triangle, and Japan will be unable to supply her armies in her newly conquered empire in China, Malaya, and the Dutch East Indies with munitions of war. The road then is open for the Chinese Army in China, for the American Navy in the Pacific, and for MacArthur to advance from his Australian stronghold all with comparatively

slight cost. . . .

'My entire above plan is simple, it has been long thought out. I have spent five years developing an air warning net and radio command service to fight this way. I have no doubt of my success.'

Wendell Wilkie delivered Chennault's note to Roosevelt who read it and passed it along enthusiastically to the War Department for consideration. The circulation of the letter at the War Department caused a major military scandal. It was already well known that Chennault and Stilwell disagreed over questions of strategy in the CBI Theatre, particularly over Stilwell's plan for a land invasion of Burma. Chennault's note, however, revealed the extent of their differences and forced Stilwell's supporters in the Pentagon to respond to Chennault's spectacular projection that the Japanese could be defeated in six months to a year if the President acceded to his suggestions.

In general, military leaders at the Pentagon reacted cooly to Chennault's air plan. Lieutenant-General Henry Arnold, Commanding General of the Army Air Force, informed General George C Marshall, Chief of Staff of the US Army, that he was opposed to seeing the China Air Task Force transformed into an independent air force under Chennault and dismissed Chennault's plan as unrealistic because of the logistical problem of supplying such an operation. Although Arnold was more than willing to concede that Chennault was an excellent tactical commander, he agreed with Stilwell and Bissell that Chennault did not fully understand the logistics of supply and, therefore, he recommended that the CATF be kept under the command of the Tenth Air Force.

In addition to General Arnold's criticism of the Chennault plan on logistical grounds, General Marshall posed other critical questions. If Chennault initiated an aggressive programme against the Japanese,

would they retaliate? If so, were the Chinese prepared to defend Chennault's airfields? Like Stilwell, Marshall did not doubt the ability and efficiency of Chennault's men but he did question the capacity of Chinese armies to withstand successfully a Japanese attack on CATF installations, which would inevitably follow any increase in aerial activity against them. If the bases of the CATF fell, all aerial operations in China might be brought to an end. Thus, as far as Marshall was concerned, until the Chinese Army was capable of protecting Chennault's air bases, CATF activities would have to be limited.

Marshall discussed his reservations about the Chennault plan with Roosevelt in December 1942. By that time, however, Roosevelt was leaning increasingly toward Chennault's position and informed Marshall that he believed that Chennault should receive an independent command in China and that he should be immediately provided with a force of a hundred planes with which he might undertake the bombing of Japanese installations and shipping in China. Roosevelt also favoured Chennault's plan – if for no other reason than for its possible psychological effect on the Japanese.

Roosevelt's increasing tendency toward implementation of Chennault's scheme reflected the tremendous influence of Chennault's lobby in Washington which included among its membership such presidential intimates as Harry Hopkins, Vice President Henry Wallace, Chinese Ambassador T V Soong, and presidential adviser Lauchlin Currie. These men consistently promoted Chennault's plan and presented Roosevelt with regular appreciative evaluations of his strategy. At the same time, they lost no opportunity to criticise Stilwell and exploit his growing rift with Chiang Kai-shek.

Stilwell was never able to counter effectively Chennault's supporters in Washington. Although he had con-

Lieutenant-General Henry H Arnold,
Commanding General of the Army Air
Force (far left), with Chennault,
Stilwell, and Sir John Dill at a
Flying Tigers base in China

siderable support from General Marshall and other military leaders, Stilwell's image at the White House steadily deteriorated. As a result, he and his supporters were placed on the defensive, attempting to justify their policies in the face of increasing criticism from Chennault's proponents and the press.

In part, Stilwell's problem reflected the difficulty of his mission. Undoubtedly, his assignment was the most delicate diplomatic mission thrust on a professional soldier during the war. Stilwell was forced to play several roles in China: he was at one and the same time Commanding General of American forces in the CBI theatre, Chief of Staff of the Chinese Army, director of the lend-lease programme in China and American representative in the SEAC command. Such a multiplicity of duties doomed Stilwell from the beginning but none more than his position as Chiang Kai-shek's Chief of Staff.

Stilwell was not the sort of man that the Chinese situation required. He had difficulty in handling the representatives of other nationalities tactfully and could not cope with the political problems he faced in China. Had he been solely a military commander, he might have been successful. On the contrary, however, he was as much a diplomat in China as a strategist. To this his temperament was not suited.

When Marshall asked Stilwell to go to China, he knew that Stilwell was not a diplomat but hoped that his knowledge of China might enable him to rally dissident political factions and increase the capabilities and efficiency of the Chinese Army. Such was not to be the case. Stilwell's attempt to revitalise the Chinese

87

Army ultimately led to his recall in 1944 and contributed substantially to his difficulties with Chennault.

Given his experience in China as a military attaché at the American embassy, Stilwell was distrustful of the leadership of the Kuomintang and insisted that the Generalissimo give him *carte blanche* as his Chief of Staff to reorganise the Chinese Army. This the Generalissimo refused to do. Although Chiang Kai-shek appreciated the need for a strong effective army, he feared the political repercussions that a reorganisation of the Chinese Army was likely to yield and refused to accede to Stilwell's demands. Above all, Chiang wished to preserve his command intact and hold his forces in reserve for the post-war battle with the Chinese communists which he believed was inevitable. Thus, when Chennault proposed his air plan in October 1942, which offered an alternative to Stilwell's plans, Chiang became its principal adherent.

In a cable sent to Roosevelt on 9th January 1943, Chiang Kai-shek expressed his support of Chennault's plan in the following manner:
'The remarkable potentialities of an air offensive in China have already been demonstrated by a small and ill-supported force. I believe that an early air offensive is feasible, since, owing to the peculiar tactical conditions which prevail here, neither the supply, material, and personnel requirements are such as to embarass the United Nations air effort elsewhere. The return, I predict, will be out of proportion to the investment, and by further weakening the Japanese air arm and striking at the sea-borne communications with their new conquests, an air offensive in China will directly prepare for the ultimate offensive we are looking for.'

In the same cable, Chiang expressed his reservations about Stilwell's plan for an invasion of Burma to re-open the Burma Road and announced his unwillingness, at that time, to commit large numbers of Chinese troops to such a scheme.

As might be expected, Stilwell did not accept Chiang's position without a struggle. On the contrary, he mounted a propaganda campaign of his own through his associates at the Pentagon. Stilwell suggested to Marshall that if Chiang did not accede to his demands voluntarily, a *quid pro quo* policy toward the Generalissimo should be adopted, and military aid to the Chinese withheld until Chiang agreed to cooperate. It was Stilwell's belief that China's total dependence on the United States gave the US sufficient leverage over the Kuomintang to force its leaders into accepting his views, views which were also shared by most high-ranking officers at the Pentagon.

Stilwell believed that strong-armed tactics were the only way of dealing with the Chinese and stated so both publically and privately. In his notes to Marshall, he repeated this view many times. According to Stilwell in order to carry out his mission of increasing the combat efficiency of the Chinese Army, a *quid pro quo* policy was absolutely essential. Logic, reasoning, and personal persuasion would do no good. Pressure was the only effective technique in dealing with the Generalissimo. 'For everything we do for him,' said Stilwell, 'we should exact a commitment from him'. This view was shared by many others in China but, unfortunately for Stilwell, not by Roosevelt's White House intimates.

Stilwell's *quid pro quo* policy was pursued with tactlessness which eventually cost him his position. His acid comments on Chiang Kai-shek and his government, which were as well known in Chungking as at the Pentagon, aroused an emotional reaction from the Kuomintang which emasculated any remaining influence Stilwell had at the White House, where Roosevelt's advisers were

**Washington, spring 1943. Allied leaders at the Trident Conference where Chennault and Stilwell present their rival plans to Roosevelt**

openly critical of him and suggested his recall.

Stilwell's advocacy of a *quid pro quo* policy actually weakened his position in China. Whatever goodwill existed between him and the Generalissimo evaporated in the debate over Chennault's plan. Chiang had little trouble in making Stilwell's position untenable, particularly in so far as Roosevelt had refused to agree to a *quid pro quo* formula in dealing with him. Turning his nearly total dependence on the United States into a position of political strength by taking advantage of the important role that Roosevelt had assigned to China in the defeat of the Japan and the postwar world, Chiang Kai-shek used his diplomatic genius to pursuade Roosevelt to favour the Chennault plan and

the idea of increased aid to China. Indeed, it might well be said that whereas Stillwell had failed in his bid to force the Chinese into acceptance of his views through the application of the *quid pro quo*, Chiang was able to apply the same principle successfully in his dealings with Stilwell and Roosevelt.

President Roosevelt ultimately acceded to Chiang Kai-shek's suggestion that Chennault be given an augmented force and an independent command in China. In March 1943 he decided to overrule his military advisors and prepared a cable to the Generalissimo, announcing his intention to place Chennault in command of a new air unit in China and to build this unit up to a strength of 500 planes as soon as conditions permitted and the Hump lift could be increased to support such an operation: In explaining his decision to Marshall, Roosevelt pointed out that Stilwell did not fully appreciate the potential of air power in

China or Chiang's commitment to the Chennault plan. Moreover, in so far as the maintenance of good Sino-American relations was involved, Roosevelt told Marshall that he had no choice but to submit to Chiang's request. At the same time, Roosevelt warned Marshall that Stilwell was using the wrong approach in dealing with Chiang and might have to be removed if he continued to treat the Generalissimo in a high handed way.

Chennault was promoted to the rank of Major-General on 3rd March 1943 and placed in command of the newly created Fourteenth Air Force (formerly the CATF) on 11th March. According to Roosevelt's instructions to Marshall, Chennault was to be given complete control over all aerial operations in China and Stilwell was to be informed that he was not to interfere with Chennault in any manner that was likely to anger Chiang Kai-shek. Although Stilwell, as American Commander-in-Chief in the

**Chennault claims that the Chinese army will adequately defend airbases in China**

CBI theatre, was to continue to direct the air ferry route over the Hump, he was to allocate sufficient tonnage to Chennault to facilitate his operations while, at the same time, leaving enough free for land operations in China and Burma.

In acceding to Chennault and Chiang, Roosevelt did not entirely abandon the idea of a second campaign in Burma. On the other hand, since it was clear that the air ferry could not support both a land operation into Burma and Chennault's air offensive in China, Roosevelt's decision created a dilemma which was bound to exacerbate the difference between Stilwell and Chennault. As might be expected, Stilwell was reluctant to see Chennault receive the lion's share of Hump supplies because that would effectively cancel his plans for a Burma campaign. Chennault, for his part,

**Pilots check in after hazardous haul over the Hump**

believed that Stilwell would continue to frustrate his plans by manipulating supply quotas but did not let this stop him from preparing additional facilities for his campaign against Japanese shipping and military installations. Thus, his requests for supplies increased markedly in April and May 1943. Since the amount of supplies flown over the Hump decreased during the same period, a crisis was reached. Clearly, one programme would have to be sacrificed. But neither Chennault nor Stilwell showed any inclination to abandon their plans, and it was Roosevelt who was forced to break the deadlock.

At the requests of Chiang Kai-shek and General Marshall, Chennault and Stilwell were called to Washington DC late in April 1943 to present their proposals to Roosevelt and other Allied leaders assembled in the capital for the Trident Conference, one of the many wartime summit strategy sessions. At this conference, both men presented their proposals and their differences were given a thorough hearing.

Chennault presented his case to Roosevelt on 30th April 1943. Once again Chennault re-stated his belief that the Japanese did not wish to engage in a major air war over China and for that reason, he told Roosevelt that every effort should be made to force them into an aerial contest. Chennault proposed to take advantage of good flying weather to launch a two month attack on Japan in July 1943 designed to wrest air superiority from them over China. In August, after this initial attack was successfully completed, Chennault proposed to move medium bombers to forward bases in east China from which they would launch a major campaign against Japanese shipping along the Yangtze

**Supplies arrive in India—Chennault is now to get the lion's share**

and in Haiphong, Hainan, and coastal ports. During September 1943, the Fourteenth Air Force would widen its activities to include Japanese shipping in the Formosa Straits and the entire Indo-China coast following which the bombers would move eastward, attacking Formosa and the Shanghai-Nanking-Hankow triangle. By the end of the year the Fourteenth Air Force would be ready to move against the Japanese Islands.

To accomplish his goals successfully, Chennault outlined his minimal requirement to Roosevelt. He would need seventy-four P-40s, seventy-five P-51s, thirty-five B-24s, forty-eight B-25s and some photo reconnaissance planes. To supply this armada, he would need some 4,790 tons of supplies per month from July to September and 7,129 tons per month thereafter. If such aid was forthcoming, Chennault assured Roosevelt that the Japanese would withdraw from their Yangtze bases and the Fourteenth Air Force could destroy a minimum of 500,000 tons of Japanese shipping in six months. If he received 10,000 tons of supply per month, Chennault guaranteed that he could destroy more than 1,000,000 tons of shipping during the same period. When asked by Roosevelt about the possibility of a Japanese attack on his forward bases, Chennault assured Roosevelt that the Chinese Army could protect his installations. When queried about the problem of supplying his forward bases he replied in the same optimistic fashion, once again assuring the President that the Chinese could handle the problem of moving supplies from Yunnan to his forward bases.

Roosevelt's reaction to Chennault's presentation was favourable, although he made no final decision until seeing General Stilwell on 1st May. At this meeting, Stilwell outlined his objections to Chennault's plan, his methods of operation, and Chiang Kai-shek's failure to honour his commitments. Stilwell did not deny that opportunities for air attacks against Japanese shipping were real nor that such attacks could reap impressive benefits. What he did fear however, was that once Chennault's attacks proved sufficiently damaging, the Japanese would launch a major offensive against the bases of the Fourteenth Air Force. Unlike Chennault, Stilwell was not optimistic about the ability of the Chinese Army to stop this advance. Should Chinese resistance fail, the Japanese would surely push forward to Kunming and Chungking which would be left virtually defenceless. Only a sufficiently well trained and equipped land force could hold these centres and Stilwell did not believe that the Chinese constituted such a force. Therefore, he suggested to Roosevelt that the first priority in China should be the reorganisation of the Chinese Army followed by an offensive in Burma to re-open the Burma Road. Only after these two goals were achieved would Chennault's plan become a reality.

Stilwell told Roosevelt that reorganisation of the Chinese Army could not be completed until Chiang Kai-shek agreed to cooperate with him. He suggested to the President that Chiang Kai-shek be reminded of the reason for the American presence in China and of his agreement to furnish manpower and accept assistance in training these men. Moreover, he also suggested that Chiang be requested to use regular military channels in dealing with the Americans in China. For Stilwell, there could be no deviation from this rule. Thus, in dealing with Chennault, Chiang could not be permitted to bypass Stilwell's command nor could Chennault be allowed willfully to bypass channels and disobey orders. Above all, Stilwell believed, as he had done consistently in the past, that Roosevelt must use a strong hand in dealing with the Generalissimo. As he put it to Roosevelt: 'The only shortcut to Japan is through China. The Chinese know this and are disposed to extract from the situation every ad-

vantage possible. Unless we are prepared to accept infinite delay, they must be held to their commitments as fully as we are holding ourselves to ours.'

Despite the objections of his military advisors, Roosevelt decided in favour of Chennault's plan for an aerial offensive because he believed it promised a quick victory over Japan. Stilwell's plan to re-occupy Burma, on the other hand, would require a major commitment of American, British, and Chinese manpower and take considerably longer to execute. Moreover, since the War Department would not commit combat troops to the Burma campaign, the success of Stilwell's scheme would rest entirely with the British and Chinese, neither of whom were anxious to use their resources in Burma. Since the British did not view the liberation of Burma as a matter of first priority and Chiang Kai-shek refused to make any commitment to the operation unless the Allies did the same, Roosevelt concluded that Stilwell's plan was impractical and dismissed it.

Politically, Roosevelt felt bound to support Chiang Kai-shek and knew that he would placate the Generalissimo by supporting Chennault's plan. Once again, fear that the Chinese might pull out of the war and make a separate peace with Japan prevailed over other fears. Since the War Department wished, above all, to keep China in the war, even Chennault's critics at the Pentagon agreed that Roosevelt had little alternative than to accept the Chennault plan if only to bolster the morale of the Chungking régime. It was thus political considerations that dictated Roosevelt's decision.

But undoubtedly, personalities also played a role in determining Roosevelt's policy. Chennault presented his proposals with ardour and enthusiasm, whereas Stilwell was sullen and rude. According to Henry Stimson, Secretary of War and Stilwell's prime supporter at the White House,

Stilwell 'never really made his number with the President' and actually angered Roosevelt by suggesting that he (the President) was being 'used' by Chiang Kai-shek. In contrast to this, Chennault and Roosevelt were quite compatible.

On 3rd May 1943, consistent with his earlier actions Roosevelt formally announced his support of Chennault's programme and took the unprecedented step of inviting Chennault to communicate with him directly in order to inform him on the progress of the air offensive. In order to facilitate the achievement of Chennault's goals, he ordered a re-allocation of Hump tonnage for a six month period beginning on 1st July. During the first two months of the programme (July and August), Chennault's allocation was to be raised from 1,000 tons per month to a minimum of 4,700 tons per month. Thereafter, he was to receive an additional allocation provided the

**Engine oil for the Tigers awaits shipment in Calcutta. All supplies must be flown the last stage over the Hump**

total air ferry tonnage could be raised to 10,000 tons per month, the figure set for realisation by 1st September. The remaining tonnage (approximately 2,000 tons) was to be used for all other purposes, including Stilwell's programmes to re-equip the Chinese Army and re-occupy Burma. Stilwell was thus forced to modify both programmes substantially in favour of more modest and realistic plans while Chennault was given *carte blanche* to destroy the Japanese in six months.

But the promises made so freely by Roosevelt could not be fulfilled, and tension increased between Chennault and Stilwell, Chiang Kai-shek and Roosevelt. Stilwell clearly perceived the difficulties surrounding the situation when he said 'it was fatal to promise anything'.

# The Fourteenth Airforce 1943

Chennault's promotion and the conversion of the China Air Task Force into the Fourteenth Air Force did not result in any immediate solution to Chennault's problems. The creation of the Air Force was premature from a purely military standpoint and Chennault's plan was put into operation before its logistical requirements could be met. As a result, Chennault was unable to achieve his objective of gaining air supremacy in China within six months.

If Chennault failed to achieve his objectives, it was not so much because he lacked the equipment to do so but, rather, that he lacked sufficient fuel reserves and supplies to use what equipment he had to its greatest effect. At the heart of this dilemma was Roosevelt's failure to anticipate the marked increase in Hump tonnage when he gave Chennault the green light at the Trident Conference.

Roosevelt had promised that the Fourteenth Air Force would receive a

minimum of 4,700 tons of supplies during the months of July and August 1943. However, in July, the total tonnage carried over the Hump was some 4,500 tons, 200 tons less than Chennault's quota set by Roosevelt at the Trident Conference. Moreover, Chennault could not be given all of this since the Chinese Government and military depended upon a portion of the total supply for their very existence. By September 1943 (by which date Hump tonnage was to reach 10,000 tons and the Fourteenth Air Force was to receive 7,128 tons of this) less than 5,000 tons a month were flown into China.

As Chennault's critics had so often warned in the past, the air lift was not up to the task of ferrying sufficient quantities of material to sustain Chennault's offensive and Chinese land forces at the same time. This was not so much because of an insufficient number of planes to ferry goods from Assam to China but, rather, because of transportation bottlenecks in India, along the route leading from Calcutta to Assam.

Movement of supplies destined for China from Calcutta and Karachi to airfields in Assam from which they would be flown over the Hump to China was a slow and laborious process. Although these Indian cities were clogged with goods, rail facilities between Bengal and Assam were inadequate to carry these supplies rapidly.

But perhaps more important than the inadequate Indian railway system was the failure of the British in India to complete airfields in Assam on schedule. At the Trident Conference the British had agreed to prepare eight new aerodromes in Assam, five to be ready by 1st June 1943, and the other three to be completed by 1st

**Chinese and American officers and officials toast the commander of Fourteenth USAF. Chennault's promotion still leaves him with his problems of supply and maintenance**

October. On 1st October only two of these fields were complete. In part, the failure to complete the fields on schedule reflected climatic conditions beyond human control. Monsoon rains in Assam during the spring and summer of 1943 were particularly heavy, even for a region noted for heavy rainfall. Because of the rains, it was impossible to utilise heavy construction equipment efficiently. However, even if the weather had been better, it is doubtful that the fields could have been completed on schedule since the British lacked sufficient heavy equipment for all their projects.

Of the two fields completed by 1st October, only one had paved runways. Thus only one field was available for the heavy transports and bombers being used to carry supplies to China and, furthermore, this field was only three hours removed from Japanese bases and subject to frequent attack.

Despite setbacks and delays in receiving supplies and equipment the Fourteenth Air Force gradually changed from a guerilla force to a fully fledged air force with area assignments under subordinate commands. Although the Fourteenth Air Force remained the smallest Army Air Force unit overseas, it covered the largest area of any air force including all of China along and south of the Yangtze as well as Burma, Thailand, Indo-China, and the Formosa straits, a formidable assignment.

Until the arrival of additional aircraft in May 1943, the Fourteenth Air Force continued to operate in the fashion of its predecessors, the CATF and the AVG, carrying on the spirit and tactics of the original Flying Tigers. In March and April 1943 bad weather and shortages of fuel restricted their activities to two offensive raids, one on 8th April against targets in Indo-China, and the other, on 24th April, against the Namtu mines in Burma.

The Japanese, on the other hand, suffered from no such shortages of fuel and supplies and took advantage of the lull in Fourteenth Air Force activities to launch a series of raids against American bases in China. These raids proved to be quite costly. For the first time in the war, the Japanese were able to pass through the air warning system without detection. Thus, on 26th April, Japanese planes ran a successful raid against the Fourteenth Air Force field at Yunnani, catching twenty P-40s on the ground, destroying two of them and damaging the others. On 28th April, similar raids were sent against Kunming and Lingling. Only the high winds and bad weather spared

these fields from the same damage the Japanese had wrought at Yunnani.

In May, the first reinforcements, the 308 Air Bombardment Group, reached the Fourteenth Air Force in China. With the arrival of this group of thirty-five B-24s, the Fourteenth Air Force possessed the capacity to strike against all Japanese installations in China, Indo-China, Burma, and Thailand from their forward bases. Although operated from tactical bases in China 1,000 miles removed from their supply bases in India, it was anticipated that the B-24s would not impose an additional strain, at least initially, on the already meagre resources of the Fourteenth Air Force since the planes could double as transports, hauling their own bombs and fuel.

The 308 Bombardment Group made its debut on 4th May, when eighteen of the 'Liberators' and twelve B-25s, accompanied by twenty-four fighters, ran a raid against targets along the Red River in Tonkin and Hainan Island. This mission was a total success and was followed up on 8th May by a raid against the Tien Ho aerodrome outside Canton – a major facility of the Japanese Air Force in south China. During this latter raid, the bombers of the 308 Group completely destroyed the main hanger and

petrol storage tanks at the field. The 308 Bombardment Group, which had distinguished itself in these first missions under Chennault's control, eventually went on to compile an impressive wartime combat record. However, in accomplishing this feat, they took the highest combat losses of any unit of the Fourteenth Air Force in China.

The Japanese retaliated after the attacks on their installations in China and Indo-China by launching a massive attack on Fourteenth Air Force HQ at Kunming on 15th May. Once again the Japanese managed to elude Chennault's air warning network and almost succeeded in destroying the base. Their attack force of thirty bombers and forty fighters met little resistance. Only the inaccuracy of the Japanese bombardiers saved the base from complete destruction.

The 15th May attack on Kunming was followed by a series of Japanese raids against other Fourteenth Air Force bases during the rest of the month. This aerial offensive was co-ordinated with an abortive land offensive up the Yangtze toward Chungking, China's wartime capital, and southward into Yunnan province, the location of many of the forward bases of the Fourteenth Air Force.

By the end of May, the Japanese had moved near Changsha and dangerously close to Hengyang, one of the principal forward bases of the Fourteenth Air Force. The drive toward Chungking was also well under way. As the Japanese advanced toward the wartime capital of China, the Chinese requested air assistance. Since the Japanese troop concentrations were beyond the range of fighters flying from safe bases, Chennault, who agreed to provide air cover to the Chinese, used his B-24s against them. Flying from Chengtu and assisted by Chinese Air Force fighters, the bombers were used to strafe Japanese

**Strikes against Japanese shipping begin—and provoke heavy attacks on Flying Tiger bases in return**

positions and attack Japanese troops massing at the Yangtze gorges, in front of Chungking. The success of this operation forced the Japanese to withdraw their advance units back to fallback positions and on 2nd June, Tokyo radio announced the suspension of the operation.

For Chennault, who returned to China after the Trident Conference to witness the end of the Japanese offensive, the Japanese failure to advance corroborated his long held belief that Japanese penetrations into the interior of China, which generally followed the course of China's major rivers, could be blunted by the proper application of air power. In his first letter to Roosevelt after his return to China, Chennault stressed this fact, stating that he believed that the successful campaign against the Japanese bore out his judgement that the Japanese were unable to supply an offensive effort capable of penetrating more than a hundred miles into the interior of China in any area where they were unable to move in supplies by water and subject to attack from the air. Thus, he assured Roosevelt once more that the Japanese could not mount a successful campaign against his bases, most of which were located well beyond the 100-mile limit, after he began his offensive operations. For the time being, Chennault's critics were silenced.

In July, Chennault's long anticipated offensive against Japanese shipping and installations was begun. Although much of the equipment promised at the Trident Conference had not arrived and fuel and spare parts were still in short supply, preparations for the offensive were completed during June and the first attack on Japanese shipping along the Yangtze was launched on 1st July, followed by attacks against shipping along the estuaries of the West River near Canton and raids against Haiphong. Despite shortages of equipment and supplies, the raids were continued for the rest of the month.

The Japanese lashed back at Chennault's installations, concentrating on American fields within striking distance of the Hankow-Haiphong railway line, a principal supply artery for Japanese forces in China, trying to separate these forward bases from bases further westward. As a result of this concentrated attack, the Japanese inflicted heavy damage on the American fields at Hengyang, and Ling-ling, forcing the abandonment of the fields until they could be repaired.

The success of the Japanese attack against the forward Air Force bases forced Chennault to divert some of his men and equipment for use against the Japanese air base at Hankow. Nevertheless, in the first month of his offensive operation, his men compiled an impressive record, sinking 41,000 tons of Japanese shipping and damaging at least 35,000 tons. On the other hand, the July offensive and the Japanese counteroffensive against Fourteenth Air Force installations proved costly in terms of equipment lost and bases damaged. Since new aircraft promised for July had not yet arrived, Chennault's situation was critical. Fearing that operations against the Japanese might have to be stopped, Chennault was forced to appeal to Stilwell for more supplies and aircraft.

Stilwell had never supported Chennault's schemes and was not inclined to do so when Chennault appealed to him at the end of July. He favoured stopping all operations from the forward bases of the Fourteenth Air Force and told Chennault and Marshall as much. As far as he was concerned, Chennault's plan had failed hardly a month after it had been launched. If Chennault was to be allowed to continue, heavy reinforcements would be needed. As might be expected, Stilwell recommended against such reinforcements. In any case, Chennault's requests could not be honoured. For the time being, he would have to make do with whatever equipment he had.

During the first two weeks of the month, bad weather forced a postponement of strikes against Japanese shipping, but on 17th August, following a break in the Monsoon rains, Haiphong was successfully attacked. Four days later, a second force was sent over Haiphong. This time, however, heavy losses were suffered when the B-24 bombers failed to rendezvous with their fighter escort. During the raid two of the original fourteen B-24s were lost and another ten badly damaged. Similar losses were sustained late in the month during an attack on Hankow during which five B-24s were lost and fifty airmen killed.

By the end of the summer, the Fourteenth Air Force had destroyed 153 Japanese aircraft at a cost of twenty-seven of their own. But Chennault realised that he could not afford to

A USAF gunner shows scars near his turret, mementos of interception by a Zero

sustain even these comparatively small losses. The Japanese were able to replace lost equipment and men with little difficulty, Chennault could not do the same.

By September, Chennault was quite disheartened. After two months of offensive operations, the Fourteenth Air Force did not have the air superiority in China its commander had hoped to achieve and with Chennault's absolute priority on Hump tonnage due to expire on 31st October, time was running short. Chennault accordingly wrote to Roosevelt, informing the President that he might have to cancel his aggressive programmes if he did not receive the equipment and supplies he had been promised at the Trident Conference. According to Chennault his failure to achieve the goals agreed to at that conference was due solely to the failure of his colleagues and superiors to meet quotas set by Roosevelt in May 1943. Although Chennault did not accuse Stilwell of sabotaging his effort, he left no doubt that Stilwell was doing little to facilitate it.

Chennault's complaints to F. D. R. were echoed by Madame Chiang and T V Soong. Their lobbying on Chennault's behalf lent additional weight to his appeal and forced the President to respond to the problem. On 16th September, Stilwell delivered a personal apology from the President to Generalissimo and Madame Chiang for the failure of the American command to deliver equipment and supplies promised to Chennault at the Trident Conference. Roosevelt assured them that reinforcements were on the way. A similar assurance was given to T V Soong on 27th September. To be sure that the equipment would reach Chennault, Roosevelt instructed General Marshall to supervise the supply operation personally.

At the beginning of October, Chennault's equipment problem was partially resolved by the transfer of two fighter squadrons from the Tenth Air Force command in Delhi to the Fourteenth Air Force command at Kunming. The arrival of these planes from India made it possible to provide temporary protection for the forward bases of the Air Force while, at the same time, providing protective cover to bombing raids which were reviewed in earnest during October. The supply problem however, still remained critical as the supplies and replacement planes promised by Roosevelt in September failed to arrive.

The failure of the Americans to deliver the goods that Roosevelt had personally promised the Generalissimo prompted the Chungking government to send a strong protest to Washington at the end of October pointing to the Allies' failure to honour commitments made at the Trident Conference. Upon receipt of this note, Roosevelt, who was constantly plagued by the failure of the military to meet its obligations in China, sent a very strong note to Marshall indicating his disgust with the matter. As he told Marshall, 'Everything seems to go wrong. But the worst thing is that we are falling down on our promises every single time. We have not fulfilled one of them. . . .' Once again he instructed Marshall to give the matter of supply to the Fourteenth Air Force his personal attention. Moreover, he also moved to correct the situation in China by cabling Churchill and asking the Prime Minister to intervene directly to facilitate the completion of aerodromes in Assam which would ease ATC operations over the Hump and allow delivery of all equipment and supplies promised to Chennault.

**Fliers arrive in India for the China-Burma theatre. Continuing supply problems mean they may find nothing to fly**

Roosevelt made it clear to Churchill that this was a matter of first priority which would lead to a major diplomatic problem if left unresolved.

If Roosevelt was concerned about the failure to deliver supplies and equipment to Chennault, for Chennault, the matter was even more critical. If supplies did not reach China quickly, the projected Burma campaign (Project Anakim) would deprive the Fourteenth Air Force of sufficient supplies to continue its offensive. Chennault therefore drafted a revised proposal and sent it to Roosevelt in October, hoping that the President would grant his priority over Hump tonnage some continuance after 31st October.

Chennault's revised plan proposed a new timetable to wrest air superiority from the Japanese but his goals remained the same. China would be divided for operational purposes into two zones, eastern and western, divided by the 108th meridian. Since

**General Stratemeyer, AAF commander in the CBI area, has bad news for Chennault: his equipment and supplies priority is withdrawn**

the weather in these two zones varied, from January to June 1944, when the weather would be good in the west, the Fourteenth Air Force would fly most of its missions in this area in support of the Burma campaign and the Hump operation. From July to December, when the weather grew steadily worse in west China, operations would be switched to the east where the Fourteenth Air Force would finally win air superiority over the Japanese and destroy Japanese shipping. To accomplish these ends, Chennault proposed a monthly supply quota of some 9,000 tons to be divided between bases in the two zones in China. In addition, he hoped to accumulate a reserve of 20,000 tons of supplies at his forward bases before beginning his offensive in east China in July 1944. If these conditions could be met, he promised that air superiority would be assured.

Chennault once again dismissed the possibility of a successful Japanese ground attack on his air bases in response to a new offensive. He based this view on the effectiveness of the Fourteenth Air Force in blunting the Japanese drive toward Chungking in June 1943. The Japanese had never successfully penetrated Chinese territory more than a hundred miles beyond their supply lines. Chennault saw little reason why they should be able to do so in the future. Since his force could successfully interdict Japanese supply routes, Japanese penetration of his east China bases could hardly be successful. Moreover, should the enemy attempt to interrupt his proposed offensive, ships carrying personnel and equipment for such an effort would be exposed to land based bombardment. Furthermore, by launching a counteroffensive in China, the Japanese would be forced to abandon essential commitments elsewhere.

Stilwell's view of the situation was somewhat different. He did not accept the validity of Chennault's forecast that the Japanese could not launch

an offensive against him. Moreover, even if the Japanese did not launch an attack on Chennault's bases, all the Fourteenth Air Force was able to do was to knock down a few Japanese planes. The Japanese would still remain in China and in force. Thus, Stilwell against acceding to Chennault's scheme and passed his recommendation along to General Marshall and President Roosevelt.

On 16th November 1943, General George Stratemeyer, Commander of the Army Air Force in the CBI theatre, replied to Chennault's plan on behalf of General Marshall and the Army. Chennault and his staff officers were praised for their carefully worked out and detailed presentation, but the substance of Chennault's plan was vetoed on the grounds that the Army was not yet in a position logistically to support it. Chennault was told that his priority on Hump supplies, which had expired in October 1943, could not be renewed. To make matters worse, Stratemeyer told Chennault that he might expect less

**The Cairo Conference of November 1943. Roosevelt's meeting with Chiang Kai-shek confirms his changed attitude to Chennault**

than he had received before the Trident Conference if Stilwell went ahead with his plan to reallocate much of the tonnage the Fourteenth Air Force had received or been promised to the Chinese Army in preparation for their role in the Burma campaign.

Stratemeyer's memo to Chennault also contained information about Operation 'Twilight', the Allied plan to place B-29 bombers in China under a command separate from the Fourteenth Air Force for the purpose of launching raids against the Japanese islands in 1944. This news came as quite a shock to the commander of the Fourteenth Air Force who had long planned to cap his career in China by serving as the architect of the aerial destruction of Japan. Chennault immediately understood that his action spelled the end of the priority of his air operations in

'Siamese twin' Tiger; P-38 Lightnings took part in the successful Shinchiku air base raid

China. With the arrival of the B-29s, the Fourteenth Air Force would become a second priority unit limited to support of Operation 'Twilight' and raids against Japanese shipping. In short, Stratemeyer's note was a clear statement of the logistical restrictions under which Chennault would be forced to operate for the rest of the war. Unfortunately for Chennault, neither he nor his supporters were able to reverse these directives. Their Trident Conference *coup* was a one-off affair.

The fact that Chennault's revised air plan was coldly received and ultimately turned down, reflected a reversal in Roosevelt's thinking with regard to Chiang Kai-shek and the Kuomintang government in Chungking. For years Roosevelt had supported Chiang and Chennault. Contrary to the advice and opinions of his military advisers, he had given Chennault the green light to put his theories into action, if for no other reason than to acknowledge the wishes of Chiang Kai-shek. Then in November 1943 his support of Chiang and Chennault began to wane, perhaps because of Chiang's carping criticism of Stilwell and of the Allied war strategy, perhaps because of Chennault's failure to achieve anything resembling air superiority in China.

Chennault and Chiang Kai-shek made a last appeal on behalf of the plan at the Cairo Conference in November 1943, the first face to face meeting of Roosevelt and the Generalissimo, but it met with little success. Much to Chennault's chagrin, Roosevelt refused to reverse Stratemeyer's decision and accede to the Generalissimo's desires, even if this meant the end of his honeymoon with Chiang Kai-shek. For Roosevelt, the experience of dealing directly with Chiang at the Cairo Conference was undoubtedly a revelatory one; he did not

quickly forget it.

Chennault derived little satisfaction from the Cairo Conference but during his absence from China, his lieutenants launched the first Fourteenth Air Force attack on Formosa on 25th November. This raid was an unmitigated success and provided some psychological relief for Chennault after his return from Egypt. The raid was well planned and brilliantly executed. On Thanksgiving morning, a raiding party of fourteen B-25s, eight P-51s and eight P-38s took off from Sui-chuan heading for the Shinchiku aerodrome on Formosa where Fourteenth Air Force reconnaissance planes had spotted seventy-five planes on the ground the day before the raid. Flying at low altitudes across the Formosa Strait to avoid radar detection, the pilots of the Fourteenth Air Force joined by Chinese members of the Chinese American Composite Wing made one pass over the field and in less than fifteen minutes, they destroyed forty-two planes on the ground without losing one man or one plane.

The raid on Formosa had important ramifications. Unknown to Chennault or his men, the success of their attack on the Shinchiku aerodrome, more than any other action in the air war, convinced the Japanese of the necessity to eliminate Allied air power in China. The Fourteenth Air Force had already proven its effectiveness in China before the raid, but their success in permeating Japanese defences on Formosa dictated the necessity to destroy the Flying Tigers to the staff officers of the China Expeditionary Army. Accordingly, in December 1943, Lieutenant-General Shunroku Hata, Commanding officer of the China Expeditionary Army, ordered an immediate aerial offensive against American installations to be followed by a massive land offensive in east China in the spring of 1944. After less than one year of operations, the Fourteenth Air Force was to be neutralised.

# Japanese offensive in China

The activities of the Fourteenth Air Force, however limited by lack of equipment and supplies, were quite costly to the Japanese. By December 1943, the Flying Tigers were destroying over 50,000 tons of Japanese shipping per month, approximately one-third of total Japanese shipping losses per month, and making regular and increasingly daring attacks on Japanese military installations in China and Indo-China. No more merely a nuisance, the Fourteenth Air Force had become a menace which the Japanese were determined to eliminate.

Plans for Operation 'Ichigo' were first discussed in the autumn of 1943, on the eve of the Chinese offensive in northern Burma. As the plan evolved, it was expanded to include more than just an offensive against American aerial installations, but the destruction of the Fourteenth Air Force remained one of its main components. As the plan was finally formulated,

the Japanese set four goals for themselves. In addition to destroying Chennault's bases of operation from the ground, the Japanese sought to establish a reliable land transport system from northern China to Indo-China, destroy potential B-29 bases from which air raids against Japan were to be launched, and cause the Nationalist government in China to be overthrown or sue for peace with Japan by weakening its armies. This would be followed by a rapid advance into east China unimpeded by the Generalissimo's crack units who were still in Burma.

The Japanese offensive was to begin in April 1944 when Japan's North China Army was to seize control of Fourteenth Air Force forward installations in east China and take the Peiping-Honkow and Canton-Hankow railway lines after which a rendezvous would be made in the Canton area with the Southern Army, operating from Indo-China. Following the rendezvous of these two armies, the second part of the Japanese offensive would be launched by a concentrated drive into Yunnan and Szechwan provinces, the strongholds of the Kuonuntang. It was expected that the operation would take five months to complete.

In preparation for Operation Ichigo, General Shunroka Hata's China Expeditionary Army was to be reinforced by the arrival of several divisions from Manchuria, new equipment, particularly artillery pieces from Japan, and extra stocks of ammunition and aviation fuels and lubricants. This massive build-up was to continue from January until April at which time the offensive would be officially launched. During the interim, the Japanese were to concentrate their activities on air raids against Fourteenth Air Force bases.

In February and March, 1944, Fourteenth Air Force Intelligence

**Japanese shipping losses grow unacceptable**

**Further increases in sinkings prompt
Operation 'Ichigo', designed to destroy
Fourteenth Air Force**

observed a massive build-up of Japanese forces in the area of the bend of the Yellow River and the Canton-Hong Kong area. Clearly the Japanese were going to launch a major offensive, perhaps the largest of the war. While in the past the combination of American air power and Chinese land forces had managed to blunt previous Japanese probes, Chennault now felt that the massiveness of Japanese preparations and the movement of crack Manchurian Divisions into China boded ill for the Allies. With 200,000 of the Generalissimo's best troops pledged to Stilwell's Burma campaign and fuel and ammunition in short supply, Chennault feared that the Japanese could not be stopped should they commit their total resources in China to an offensive in east China.

On the eve of the Japanese offensive, Chennault warned Chiang Kai-shek of the vulnerability of their position: 'It is unnecessary to point out that all the new military equipment brought into China during the past two years has been assigned to the Chinese Armies on the Salween Front. Both equipment and many tens of thousands of troops have actually been borrowed for the Salween front from the Chinese forces which must meet the enemy offensives in Central and East China. . . .

'Under the circumstances, therefore, it is necessary to inform your excellency that the combined air forces in China, excluding the VLR (B-29) project, may not be able to withstand the expected Japanese air offensive and will certainly be unable to afford air support to the Chinese ground forces over the areas and on the scale desired. In order to put the air forces on a footing to accomplish these measures, drastic measures must be taken to provide them with adequate supplies and adequate strength must be taken. As the Japanese threat appears to be immediate, such measures should be taken without further delay.'

In addition to warning the Generalissimo of the impending disaster in eastern China, on 6th April Chennault submitted to Stilwell a detailed statement of his logistical needs in the event of a Japanese attack. Chennault did not believe that he could fight off a Japanese attack and provide air cover for the Chinese Army at the same time, unless lines of communication between Kunming and his forward bases were improved and his quota of Hump supplies raised to 8,000-10,000 tons per month. If this was not done or if supplies destined for the B-29 squadron at Chengtu were not diverted to his units, it was Chennault's view that the security of China would be in doubt, in which case Stilwell's Burma campaign would have no chance of success.

Chennault's warnings were not well received in Chungking. Stilwell's staff officers feared that Chennault's predictions might persuade Chiang Kai-shek to withdraw his forces from the Burma operation. Considering the difficulty that Stilwell had in persuading Chiang to honour this commitment in the first place, it is not surprising that Stilwell's staff resented Chennault's interference and discounted his prediction of a major Japanese offensive.

Even if Stilwell's staff had been more willing to listen to Chennault's arguments, it is doubtful that they could have acceded to his request for supplies and maintained, at the same time, Stilwell's land offensive in Burma. Moreover, with the Japanese pressing on towards India, they were besieged with requests from Mountbatten's headquarters to divert cargo planes from the Hump run to India. Mountbatten's request for assistance clearly took precedence over Chennault's. If the Japanese pushed on to

capture ATC fields in Assam, all efforts to supply China would be frustrated. With the Burma Road still closed and the Hump lift terminated, the blockade of China would be completed. Chennault's request for additional supplies was accordingly turned down and the commander of the Flying Tigers was instructed to trim the activities of the Fourteenth Air Force to the point where he could be sure of reasonable reserves for an emergency.

Deprived of equipment and the supplies he believed necessary to hold the line against the Japanese, Chennault formulated an alternative plan – to strike against the Japanese before they struck against American installations. On the basis of Intelligence supplied to the Fourteenth Air Force by the Chinese, it was assumed that the Japanese would not initiate their land offensive until May. This being the case, Chennault proposed to move his men and equipment into positions at Chinese Air Force bases in north China within easy reach of Japanese troop concentrations along the Yellow River and launch a pre-emptive offensive late in April.

But contrary to the information passed along to Chennault in Chinese Intelligence reports, the Japanese launched their offensive in April, moving across the Yellow River at Kaifeng on the morning of 17th April and heading southwards along the railway line leading to Hankow and the Yangtze. Since preparations for the Fourteenth Air Force pre-emptive raids were incomplete and the Japanese attack was launched at least two weeks earlier than expected, the opportunity to strike before the enemy was under way was lost and during the early part of their offensive the Japanese encountered little aerial resistance.

With a large part of the resources of the Fourteenth Air Force tied down in Yunnan in support of the Burma campaign and the bases of the Chinese Air Force inadequately prepared to

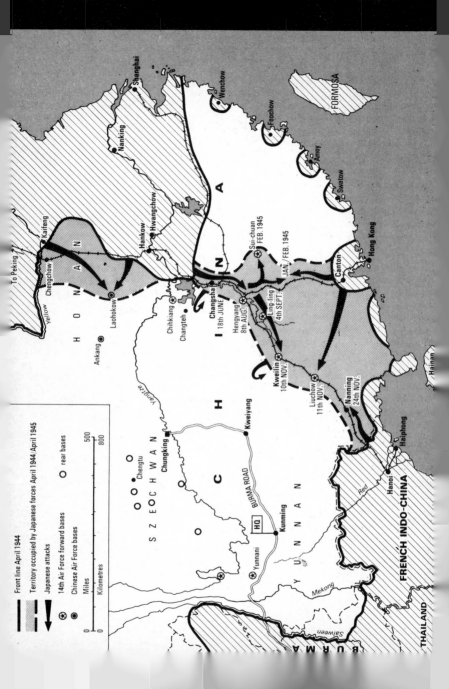

**Front line April 1944**

**Territory occupied by Japanese forces April 1944 / April 1945**

**Japanese attacks**

⊗ **14th Air Force forward bases**          ○ **rear bases**

⊙ **Chinese Air Force bases**

Miles

| 0 | 500 |

| 0 | 800 |

Kilometres

FORMOSA

Shanghai

Wenchow

Foochow

Nanking

Hwangchow

Amey

Hankow

Swatow

Kaifeng

Sui-chuan
FEB. 1945

Chengchow

To Peking ?

H O N A N

C H I N A

Canton

Hong Kong

Laohokow

Changsha
18th JUNE

JAN. / FEB. 1945

Ling-ling
4th SEPT.

Chihkiang

Changteh

Hengyang
8th AUG.

Ankang

Yellow

Kweilin
10th NOV.

Liuchow
11th NOV.

Nanning
24th NOV.

Hainan

Yangtze

Kweiyang

Haiphong

Chungking

Chengtu

S Z E O C H W A N

C H I N A

Hanoi

BURMA ROAD

Red

HQ Kunming

Y U N N A N

FRENCH INDO-CHINA

Yunnani

Mekong

Salween

B U R M A

THAILAND

receive his units, Chennault could offer little assistance to the Chinese Army. Chinese hopes of stopping the Japanese advance north of Hankow depended largely on the ability of the Fourteenth Air Force to stall the enemy, but because they had been caught off guard by the early start of the Japanese campaign the Fourteenth Air Force flew only two raids in support of the Chinese in April, neither of which was successful in slowing the advance of General Hata's 250,000 men.

The Japanese offensive in north China moved quickly. The Chinese armies, suffering from lack of equipment and inadequate leadership, were able to offer little effective resistance without aerial support. Chennault, who was ordered by Stilwell to divert several units to the protection of the B-29 installation at Chungking on 17th April, could not initially provide this support and, as a result, the Japanese quickly overran Honan province.

Chennault balked at relegating his men to the defence of Chengtu at a time when the Japanese were rapidly shattering Chinese defences in the Yangtze valley near Hankow and informed Stilwell of his conviction that air resources were being wasted in the process. Since Chengtu was not in any immediate danger, Chennault suggested that Stilwell reverse his instructions and allow the men of the Fourteenth Air Force to resume offensive operations against the Japanese. Stilwell accepted Chennault's suggestion, but in the process lost no opportunity to berate his air command in China. In answer to Chennault's plea, Stilwell replied:
'I am glad to hear that the defence of Chengtu is child's play. I had gathered from your letter of 8th April that the security of China as a base for Matterhorn (B-29 project) and other military operations against Japan might be in doubt. It is a relief to know that we have no problem at Chengtu and under these circumstances of course

the question of action in emergency will not arise. Until it does, there is no intention of limiting the scope of your operations in any way.'

Although given permission to resume operations against Japanese troops advancing toward the Yangtze, Chennault could hardly provide adequate air support for the Chinese because of the diversion of many of his planes to the Burma Campaign and the perilously low fuel reserves at the east China bases of the Fourteenth Air Force. At the time (30th April), there were 500 planes in the Fourteenth Air Force, 400 of which were operational. Of these operational craft, at least 200 were committed to the Burma Campaign, leaving another 200 planes to protect the Hump lift and supply air cover for the Chinese – a totally inadequate number of aircraft to do both jobs well. However, the shortage of supplies at the forward bases of the Fourteenth Air Force was probably more critical than the shortage of planes. The difficulty of moving supplies to these bases was compounded by the partial cutback of supplies to Chennault. As mentioned above, whereas Chennault had asked Stilwell for between 8,000-10,000 tons per month, he was actually receiving about 6,000 tons per month for all operations as of 1st May 1944.

In May, as the Japanese offensive continued, Chiang Kai-shek asked Stilwell to divert B-29 stock piles for use of the Fourteenth Air Force. When Stilwell refused to consider this transfer of supplies, Chiang, at Chennault's suggestion, appealed directly to President Roosevelt. At the time, officials at the War Department dismissed the Generalissimo's panic and Roosevelt refused either to release the B-29 stockpiles to the Fourteenth Air Force or to place Chiang, as Supreme Commander, China Theatre, in command of the B-29 unit at Chengtu. Confirming this decision to reject Chiang's requests, Stilwell received the following rationalisation of the Department's decision:

A 75mm howitzer is loaded preparatory to opening fire on the Japanese-held Pingka Valley.

'It is our view that the early bombing of Japan will have a far more beneficial effect on the situation in China than the long delay in such an operation which would be caused by the transfer of those stocks to Chennault . . . Furthermore the Twentieth Bomber Group (B-29s) must not be localised under any conditions anymore than we would localise the Pacific Fleet. Please keep this in mind.'

In mid-May, Stilwell conveyed the decision of the War Department to the Generalissimo, who at once demanded that Stilwell return from Burma to Chungking to survey the crisis in China at first hand. Undaunted by Roosevelt's initial hesitance to divert supplies from Project Matternhorn, Chiang insisted that the China crisis dictated that Stilwell override the War Department's veto of the use of B-29 stocks by Chennault. Stilwell, as Commander-in-Chief of American forces in the CBI, had the authority to use the B-29s or supplies stockpiled for them at Chengtu in case of emergency. Chiang knew this and continued to pressure Stilwell to make a decision in favour of Chennault.

Chiang Kai-shek's intransigeance placed Stilwell in an awkward position. On the one hand, he knew that President Roosevelt placed great faith in Project Matterhorn and its potential. To abort the achievement of the project's objectives or delay the project unduly would undoubtedly disturb Roosevelt and his military advisors. On the other hand, Stilwell knew that Chiang Kai-shek believed that the B-29 project was draining resources that could be used in defence of Fourteenth Air Force installations in east China, and Stilwell could ill afford to alienate the Generalissimo

by failing to give his opinions a fair hearing. Since China's continued presence in the Allied coalition against Japan was absolutely vital and there appeared to be no strong candidate the United States could support in China as an alternative to the Generalissimo should he break with the US, Stilwell was faced with a problem of major proportions. President Roosevelt had lost some of his faith in Chiang following the Cairo Conference, but having established the Generalissimo as a great Allied leader, Roosevelt could hardly afford to abandon him overnight. Both political myths in Washington and military realities in Chungking harassed Stilwell.

He could not ignore the persistent requests for supplies received almost daily from Chungking and Kunming, nor could he deny that the situation in China was grave. At the same time, however, it was his firm belief that Chennault and Chiang were primarily responsible for the east China *débacle* and he was bitter that his Burma campaign might have to be sacrificed because Chennault had misled the Generalissimo into believing that the Japanese could not successfully complete an offensive against Fourteenth Air Force installations in Yunnan and Szechwan. Although he could not refuse to come to their aid, Stilwell believed it was absolutely necessary that the Generalissimo should be forced to accept and understand the real roots of the China crisis – Chennault's strategical miscalculation and his own failure to facilitate the reform of the Chinese Army.

Stilwell felt particularly hostile towards Chennault. According to Stilwell, Chennault had assured Chiang Kai-shek that the Fourteenth Air Force could effectively prevent a Japanese offensive. When he failed in this, Stilwell accused Chennault of preparing an excuse for himself by telling the Generalissimo that if he had more supplies – supplies which he knew he would not be receiving – he

**Japanese forces quickly overcome Chinese opposition**

could halt the attack:
'He [Chennault] tries to duck the consequences of having sold the wrong bill of goods, and put the blame on those who pointed out the danger long ago and tried to apply the remedy.
He has failed to damage the Jap supply line. He has not caused any Japanese withdrawals. On the contrary, our preparations have done exactly what I prophesied, i.e. drawn a Jap reaction, which he now acknowledges the ground forces can't handle, even with the total air support he asked for and got.'
As far as Stilwell was concerned, Chiang Kai-shek would never be persuaded to recognise his past errors and agree to work cooperatively with the American command unless Chennault was removed. Stilwell consistently urged the replacement of

Chennault in his communications to General Marshall, but political factors dictated that Chennault should be retained, at least for the time being, and Stilwell had little choice but to accept this decision.

As the situation in China became increasingly grave, Stilwell left Burma for China late in May, arriving in Chungking on 5th June. In conferences with Chiang and Chennault, he was once again pressed to increase supplies to the Fourteenth Air Force and, for the first time, it was suggested that Chennault be granted temporary control of the B-29 unit at Chengtu, so that they could be used against the Japanese. Chennault and the Generalissimo were convinced that these steps were absolutely necessary and told Stilwell that since Chinese land forces could not defend Chennault's forward bases, the Fourteenth Air Force remained the only obstacle to a complete Japanese victory in China.

Despite the hostility between Stilwell and Chennault, Stilwell could see that Chennault's estimate of the impending disaster in China was correct and promised to divert Chennault's units 1,500 tons per month from supplies destined for use in Project Matterhorn. On the matter of the use of the B-29s against Japanese troop concentrations around Hankow, Stilwell did not have the authority to authorise Chennault's use of the planes but promised Chennault that he would cable the War Department for instructions on this matter.

Stilwell was not optimistic about the value of using air power against ground forces and opposed putting the VLR squadron at Chengtu under Chennault's control. Nevertheless, he had no choice but to convey Chennault's requests to Washington. As he expected, General Arnold was determined to save the B-29s for use against industrial installations in Japan and refused Chennault's request for temp-

**Warhawks landing in Upper Burma; aircraft now unavailable for the support of Chinese resisting the Japanese advance to the Yangtze**

orary use of these planes to strafe and bomb troops emplacements. Replying to Arnold's instructions, Stilwell indicated his approval of the decision to use the B-29s only against the Japanese Islands: 'Instructions understood and exactly what I hoped for. As you know, I have few illusions about power of air against ground troops. Pressure from G-MO forced the communication.'

Stilwell's arrival in Chungking and his decision to increase Chennault's supply allotment by at least 1,500 tons contributed little to stopping the Japanese advance into east China, which continued with full force in June 1944. Denied use of the B-29 squadron, Chennault's projected attack on Hankow had to be abandoned. Fourteenth Air Force activities were limited to fighter strikes and strafing runs on Japanese troop movements. Such manoeuvres proved costly and ineffective, a waste of fuel and resources. The Japanese advance contined unabated despite the efforts of the Flying Tigers which were heroic but helpless.

On 18th June 1944, the Japanese took Changsha, a major rail centre and gateway to Fourteenth Air Force installations in east China. Having taken Changsha, the Japanese moved southwards toward Hengyang, site of one of the bases of the Fourteenth Air Force and also an important railhead, one of the few remaining stops along the Hankow-Hanoi railway still held by Chinese. The defence of Hengyang was absolutely vital to Allied interests and absorbed all of the resources of the Flying Tigers and their Chinese Allies for several weeks.

As preparations were being made to defend Hengyang against the Japanese, Vice-President Henry Wallace arrived in China on 20th June. Sent to China as Roosevelt's personal emissary to survey the crisis in China, Wallace's visit, however brief, was to be one of the most controversial inspections of the war in the CBI theatre.

Wallace's visit to Chungking was first announced to Stilwell and Chennault on 19th May, a day before his arrival in China. There was thus little opportunity to provide Wallace with a detailed itinerary or to prepare for his arrival. Stilwell, who had returned to Burma, could not come back to Chungking and Wallace could not spare the time to travel to the campaign front in Burma. As a result, Wallace spent most of his time with Chiang Kai-shek and Chennault, seeing Stilwell's staff officers only briefly.

In Stilwell's absence, Chennault and Chiang had an opportunity to present their own position on the east China débacle. From the moment that Wallace arrived until his departure, they monopolised his time. And Wallace was accordingly converted to their

position, particularly with regard to the need to recall Stilwell if the China crisis was to be resolved successfully and Allied unity preserved.

It was no secret in Chungking and Washington that relations between Stilwell and the Generalissimo were strained but the depth of Chiang's antagonism toward Stilwell took Wallace somewhat by surprise. Wallace left China with the impression that the situation there demanded Stilwell's recall and prompt attention to Chennault's needs. He cabled these conclusions to Roosevelt on 26th June, shortly before leaving China.

Wallace's first inclination was to suggest Chennault as Stilwell's replacement as American Commander-in-Chief in the CBI theatre. However, after Chennault's aide, Joseph Alsop, suggested that the War Department would never approve Chennault's appointment, Wallace dropped his plan to propose Chennault's name and decided, instead to suggest

General Albert Wedemeyer as Stilwell's replacement. Although Wallace had originally thought Chennault an ideal candidate to serve as Stilwell's successor, he was not so naïve as to be blind to Chennault's limitations, and to see the significance of his poor relations with military leaders at the Pentagon. However, having decided that Chennault should not be nominated to replace Stilwell, Wallace was determined that Chennault's air programme should not be stifled by Generals Arnold and Marshall because of personality conflicts. Therefore, in his reports to the President, Wallace presented Chennault's revised plan to defeat the Japanese by December 1944.

Wallace's report to Roosevelt stirred a hornet's nest of controversy at the War Department, seat of Stilwell's staunchest supporters. The Joint Chiefs prepared to defend their colleague by preparing an alternative position paper on the situation in China, concentrating on Chiang Kai-

**Despite urgent requests, release of B-29 stockpiles for Chennault's fliers is refused**

shek's mistaken support of Chennault and the strategical and tactical naïveté of the commander of the Fourteenth Air Force. Military leaders at the Pentagon were generally agreed that Chennault's air plan and the massive supply effort to sustain it were a waste of American resources and hindered operations elsewhere. Chennault's policies were not paying dividends in China and were curtailing activities in Europe because of the diversion of supply planes and other equipment from Italy to China. This view was incorporated in the official JCS statement concerning the China crisis presented to President Roosevelt on 4th July 1944, a document which also contained the strangest statements in refutation of Chennault's theories issued during the war.

In attempting to discredit Chennault's arguments the Joint Chiefs drew on experiences in other war theatres:

'Our experience against both the Germans and Japanese in theatres where we have had immensely superior air power has demonstrated the inability of air forces alone to prevent the movement of trained and determined ground armies. If we have been unable to stop the movement of ground armies in Italy with our tremendous air power, there is little reason to believe that Chennault, with the comparatively small air force that can be supported in China, can exert a decisive effect on Japanese ground forces in China. The more effective his bombing of their shipping . . . the more determined will be the Japanese thrusts in China.'

What was needed, according to the JCS report, was a reorganisation of the Chinese Army and a fully fledged commitment of Chinese forces to stop the Japanese advance. Chennault's plan offered only pipe dreams. Time was running out and reality demanded that Stilwell be given a free hand by the Generalissimo:

'The time has come, in our opinion, when all the military power and resources remaining in China must be entrusted to one individual capable of directing that effort in a fruitful way against the Japanese. There is no-one in the Chinese Government or armed forces capable of co-ordinating the Chinese military effort in such a way as to meet the Japanese threat. During this war, there has been only one man who has been able to get Chinese forces to fight against the Japanese in an effective way. That man is General Stilwell.'

Roosevelt could hardly ignore the recommendations of his Chiefs of Staff. Accordingly, for the time being, Stilwell's position of Commander-in-Chief in the CBI was reconfirmed and all rumours of his replacement were quashed. Chennault was to be given whatever supplies could be spared but his operations were not to interfere with Stilwell's programme in Burma and the reorganisation of Chinese forces in China. To be sure the Generalissimo understood his position, Roosevelt addressed a frank note to Chiang on 6th July 1944, strongly supporting Stilwell and urging Chiang to do the same by granting him full authority to undertake a reform of the Chinese Army. Summarising his position, Roosevelt stated:

'I am promoting Stilwell to the rank of full general and I recommend for your most urgent consideration that you recall him from Burma and place him directly under you in command of all Chinese and American forces, and that you charge him with full responsibility and authority for the co-ordination and direction of the operations required to stem the tide of the enemy's advances. I feel that the case of China is so desperate that if radical and properly applied remedies are not immediately effected, our common cause will suffer a disastrous setback.'

For the moment, the Generalissimo had no choice but to accept the President's advice in principle, although in fact Chiang continued to resist placing his forces under Stilwell's thumb. For Chennault, Roosevelt's acceptance of the recommendations of the JCS marked the end of an era when the lobby of the Fourteenth Air Force in Washington was able to persuade the President to overrule the suggestions of his military advisors in favour of Chennault's unorthodox strategy and tactics. Although Stilwell would soon be recalled from China, Chennault would never again have the opportunity of putting his air plan into operation. For the remainder of the war, Fourteenth Air Force activities would largely be limited to support of ground forces in

**The ceremony of the presentation of the Distinguished Service Medal. Neither Chennault nor Stilwell trouble to pretend great friendship**

From the start of Vice-President Henry Wallace's visit to China Chennault and Chiang fill him with their version of events

the CBI theatre.

Japan's drive in China stalled before the city of Hengyang for forty-nine days during the summer of 1944. The length of the battle for Hengyang and the fierce resistance put up by Chinese forces defending the city reflected the vital location of the city and the absolute necessity of holding it if the Japanese offensive was to be turned back. Hengyang was located at the centre of the Hankow-Hanoi axis, along the main line of communication between Indo-China and Japanese occupied China. Given the effectiveness of Fourteenth Air Force raids against Japanese shipping, control of Hengyang and the rail facilities between Haiphong and Hankow was absolutely necessary for the Japanese if they were to continue to sustain

their armies in China. Thus, the Battle for Hengyang became one of the major Sino-Japanese confrontations of the war.

Hengyang was defended by Chinese troops under the command of General Hsueh Yueh, a Cantonese and one of the most capable Chinese officers in the Generalissimo's army. He commanded a force of about forty divisions, poorly equipped and badly in need of arms and ammunition, but well disciplined and dedicated to the defence of China. Hsueh was assisted in the defence of Hengyang by several fighter squadrons of the Fourteenth Air Force based at the Hengyang aerodrome and nearby fields. Together, these Chinese and Americans withstood the attack of their adversaries for seven weeks.

The Japanese began their attack on Hengyang on 28th June 1944, ten days after their capture of Changsha. During the first two weeks of the contest for Hengyang, the Japanese made little headway, largely due to the effectiveness of Fourteenth Air Force missions against them. Although the Fourteenth Air Force did not ultimately succeed in halting the Japanese advance, they did slow it down substantially. Their attacks on railway facilities and highways leading to Hengyang brought Japanese supply operations to a crawl. Due to daylight raids against their supply routes, goods had to be carried by truck convoys travelling only late at night. The result was that men and equipment could only be moved to the battle front at a snail's pace.

After two weeks of daily attacks on Japanese supply lines, planes of the Fourteenth Air Force had to be grounded because of lack of fuel. From 12th to 24th July, almost all air operations against the Japanese were halted. During this interim, the Japanese were able to move in supplies and additional men, thus tightening their noose around Hengyang.

The Chinese defenders under Hsueh Yueh's Lieutenant-General Fong Hsien-chien, fought valiantly to retain the citadel but ultimately were forced to retreat from Hengyang. Although the Fourteenth Air Force flew some 4,454 sorties against the Japanese in support of the Chinese garrison at Hengyang between 28th June and 1st August, Hengyang fell to the Japanese on 8th August 1944.

The fall of Hengyang was hastened by the inability of the Fourteenth Air Force to provide sustained air coverage for the Chinese and American air bases at Lingling and Kweilin, the next stops along the railway line leading from Hankow to Hanoi. Both of these bases had been important forward installations of the Fourteenth Air Force from which the Flying Tigers had flown countless missions

**Stilwell's replacement, Major-General Wedemeyer, cordially greeted by Chennault**

**Civilians flee Kweilin by rail as Japanese threaten to overrun the town and Fourteenth AF base**

against the Japanese. Now, after three years of warfare, the Japanese were poised to take these fields.

Although Chennault had been granted an additional supply allocation in July, these supplies did not reach the forward areas until the beginning of September, by which time the Japanese had taken Lingling (4th September) and were advancing toward Kweilin. Since there was little chance of stopping the Japanese advance, preparations were made to evacuate Fourteenth Air Force installations in the path of the Japanese offensive.

By the middle of September, the situation facing Chennault was more critical than any he had faced since

the Japanese invasion of Burma in 1942. As the Japanese marched toward Kweilin, he and leaders of the Chinese government asked for emergency rations of gasoline and other supplies, hoping to be able to stall the Japanese before Kweilin until Chinese reinforcements could be sent to that city. Their request was made through the office of General Stilwell.

Stilwell received Chennault's request for emergency aid coldly. As far as he was concerned, the situation in east China was hopeless and to commit any additional resources to Chennault would only compound the disaster. What was needed, he believed was a major commitment on the part of Chiang Kai-shek to reorganise his land forces under Stilwell's command. Therefore, Stilwell replied to Chennault's request in the negative, hoping to use the east China crisis as a lever

to force the Generalissimo to recognise the realities of the military situation in China. Unfortunately for him, the Generalissimo viewed this failure to recognise Chennault's plea as a deliberate attempt to sabotage the east China campaign in favour of continuing the reconquest of Burma. This belief soon led Chiang to demand Stilwell's recall.

Stilwell's refusal to come to the rescue of Chennault was based on his long held view of the limited potential of air power and a personal assessment of the situation in China. After receiving Chennault's desperate warnings, Stilwell temporarily divorced himself from the campaign in Burma to visit the front in China. On 14th September, Stilwell flew to Kweilin where he made an inspection of preparations for the defence of that city and the Fourteenth Air Force aerodrome there. His observations confirmed his conviction that the situation was grave and could not be

**Despite the triumphant message of the wall-chart, Chennault is desperate for supplies**

remedied by applying 'band-aids to open wounds'.

Following his return from Kweilin, Stilwell returned to Chungking to confer with Chiang Kai-shek. He found the Generalissimo agitated over his refusal to aid Chennault and ready to pull his troops out of Burma if that was necessary to save the situation in China. Sensing the Generalissimo's anger, Stilwell said little to Chiang but informed Marshall after his meeting with Chiang that it was time for some 'plain talk' with T V Soong to resolve the growing impasse between himself and Chennault and Chiang. Marshall not only concurred with Stilwell's suggestions, he also took the initiative to write a blunt note to the Generalissimo which was revised by the President and delivered to Chiang on 19th September.

**Stilwell in Burma is unsympathetic; visiting the front in China convinces him of the gravity of the situation**

In his note to the Generalissimo, the President once again stressed the urgency of placing Stilwell in command of Chinese forces if a disaster in China was to be averted:
'I have urged time and again in recent months that you take drastic action to resist the disaster which has been moving closer to China and to you. Now, when you have not yet placed General Stilwell in command of all forces in China, we are faced with the loss of a critical area in east China with possible catastrophic consequences. . .
Even though we are ralling the enemy back in defeat all over the world this will not help the situation in China for a considerable time. The advance of our forces across the Pacific is swift. But this advance will be too late for China unless you act now and vigorously. Only drastic and immediate action on your part alone can be in time to preserve the fruits of your long years of struggle and the efforts

we have been able to make to support you. Otherwise political and military considerations alike are going to be swallowed in military disaster.'

Roosevelt's message was personally delivered to the Generalissimo by Stilwell, who stood by as Chiang read the Chinese translation of the text of the note. Chiang's immediate public reaction to the note was to state that he understood the President and dismiss the gathering. Unknown to Stilwell and other American officials, the Generalissimo fumed over the ultimatum sent to him from Washington.

Chiang Kai-shek responded to Roosevelt's note on 25th September 1944, six days after receiving it. For the first time, the depth of the Generalissimo's hostility toward Stilwell was made clear to the President in no uncertain terms. Chiang pointed out that Stilwell had repeatedly failed to co-operate with him and there was no reason to believe that after two and a half years Stilwell was likely to change. To appoint Stilwell as his field commander would be to 'knowingly court inevitable disaster'. Even worse, it would do irreparable damage to vital Sino-American military co-operation. Although Chiang stated that he was not opposed to the idea of an American officer serving as his field commander, under no circumstances would he accept Stilwell in this role. 'I cannot,' said Chiang, 'confer this heavy responsibility upon General Stilwell, and will have to ask for his resignation as chief of staff of the China Theatre and his relief from duty in this area.'

Chiang's message to Roosevelt created a crisis in Washington which

**Their mutual regard unshaken by Roosevelt's attitude and the hostility of Stilwell, Chiang and Chennault shake hands after the latter's decoration with the highest award ever given to a foreigner: The 'Order of the Blue Sky and White Sun'**

General Stilwell back in the States, recalled on Chiang Kai-shek's insistence

threatened to disrupt the Allied effort in China. Stilwell's supporters at the War Department immediately rallied behind their colleague and attempted to persuade the President to support him even at the risk of shattering the Sino-American alliance. General Marshall urged Roosevelt to force Chiang to accept Stilwell as his field commander or face the loss of American aid and military assistance. Marshall believed that if the President made it clear that he was not prepared to continue supporting the Chungking régime unless the Generalissimo buried the hatchet with Stilwell, Chiang would have no choice but to accept Stilwell. Secretary of War, Henry L Stimson agreed with Marshall and went one step further, suggesting to Roosevelt that if Stilwell were recalled a grave injustice would be done which would preclude

an effective relationship between Chiang and any individual sent to China to replace Stilwell. Summarising the positions of many at the Pentagon, Stimson lamented Roosevelt's failure to support Stilwell against Chiang and Chennault, who Stimson believed had been used by Chiang as a pawn to extract the maximum aid from the US with a minimum commitment from his régime. According to Stimson, America's continuous support of the Chungking régime and Chennault's schemes were crippling programmes in other war theatres and paying no dividends in China where the situation worsened daily. If Stilwell was to be recalled, any likelihood of a military victory in China would be eliminated. With his exit from China, even worse failures would befall the Chinese and America's military investment would have been for naught.

Roosevelt could hardly ignore the strong views of his military advisers

concerning the Stilwell affair. To do so would have destroyed the confidence of these men in their commander-in-chief which was absolutely necessary for the continued efficient conduct of the war. On the other hand, Roosevelt hesitated to take measures likely to hasten his break with the Generalissimo. The Sino-American alliance was dear to Roosevelt's heart and although he had lost considerable faith in Chiang Kai-shek, the President was not ready to dissolve the Chinese-American partnership if it was still possible to keep it alive by effecting a compromise settlement with Chiang. It was toward this kind of compromise that Roosevelt worked in preparing his answer to Chiang's message.

In coming to grips with the China *débâcle* Roosevelt perceived that changing circumstances in the course of the war against Japan had led to a new situation in which China was not necessarily as important a factor in

**Major-General Hurley, (centre) one of those accused by Stilwell in his diaries of being agents of his downfall**

the defeat of the Japanese as had once been assumed. China was no longer, according to the JCS, a primary factor in American plans for defeating Japan. If this was the case, it might be possible to resolve the Stilwell affair by relieving Stilwell of his China command while allowing him to continue the Burma campaign. Stilwell would not necessarily have to be replaced in China since whatever happened there was not likely to alter the course of Japan's defeat. This plan had the merits of placating the Generalissimo while allowing Stilwell to complete his mission in Burma and Roosevelt found in this solution the compromise he was seeking.

Roosevelt replied to Chiang Kai-shek's demand that Stilwell be recalled on 5th October. In his note to the Generalissimo, the President an-

131

nounced his surprise and regret over Chiang's decision that Stilwell would have to be relieved of his duties in China but did not argue with the Generalissimo's request that Stilwell be relieved as his Chief of Staff. Going even further, Roosevelt suggested that Stillwell might also be relieved of responsibility for the lend-lease program in China. However, Roosevelt was of the opinion that Stilwell should be retained as commander of Chinese ground troops in Burma and Yunnan and should continue to direct the Hump lift. If these conditions were satisfactory to the Generalissimo, Roosevelt promised to appoint another American officer to advise him at an early date. At the end of his message, Roosevelt asked Chiang for an immediate reply and stressed the necessity of allowing Stilwell to complete the Burma campaign.

Four days after receiving Roosevelt's compromise proposition, Chiang issued his reply to General Patrick Hurley ,Roosevelt's emissary in Chungking. His answer to Roosevelt was explicitly negative and blunt in the extreme:

'So long as I am Head of State and Supreme Commander in China, it seems to me that there can be no question as to my right to request the recall of an officer in whom I can no longer repose confidence. . . .

'Both the President and the War Department are dependent on General Stilwell for information concerning the military situation in China. Thus the President may not be aware that I not only have no confidence in General Stilwell, but also lack confidence in his military judgment. . . . Whatever my opinion of General Stilwell as a man maybe, I might bring myself to appoint him to command in China if I thought well of him as a military leader. However, with all the facts before me I have come to the conclusion that he is not competent to envisage or to deal with a problem of such range and complexity as now confronts us.'

Chiang refused to consider Roosevelt's proposition that Stilwell be retained in Burma, commenting that if Stilwell was incompetent to continue his command in China, there was little reason to assume he would be any more competent in Burma. The answer, Chiang suggested, was to replace Stilwell with an American officer with whom he could work cooperatively to reverse the military crisis in east China and achieve a final victory against Japan.

Chiang Kai-shek's adamance left Roosevelt with no alternative but to recall Stilwell. This was accomplished on 18th October 1944, when the President relieved Stilwell of all obligations in the CBI theatre and arranged for his transfer to a desk job at the Pentagon. At the same time, the President appointed General Albert Wedemeyer to command American forces in the China theatre.

Stilwell's recall represented a diplomatic triumph for Chiang and Chennault, their last of the war. After years of bickering over the potential of air power versus land power and the problems posed by supplying his operations in China, Chennault was rid of Stilwell. As events were to prove, however, Stilwell's recall provided no immediate solution to Chennault's problems. On the contrary, in many respects, Stilwell's recall marked the beginning of the end of the Fourteenth Air Force in China. During his remaining tenure in China, events rapidly passed Chennault by and he retired from China no more gloriously than Stilwell.

Whatever his fortunes after Stilwell's recall, Chennault was as much responsible for his superior's recall as any man in China, including Chiang Kai-shek. Had he not provided the Generalissimo with a convenient pawn to be used to resist reform of the Chinese Army and Government, it is doubtful that the Generalissimo could have engineered Stilwell's demise as readily as he did. Although Chennault was by no means consciously

as the Generalissimo's dupe, he
...ly into Chiang's trap by failing
...o discriminate between Stilwell, his
avowed opponent, and Chiang, who
was really the source of many of his
problems. In fairness to Chennault
and the proponents of an air strategy
in China, however, it must be said
that much of the dilemma they faced
was neither of their making or Stilwell's. At least in part, Roosevelt's
predilection for a 'quick' victory over
the Japanese and his near obsession
with the role of China among the
powers lay at the root of the *débacle* in
China. Both Stilwell and Chennault
fell victim to these fantasies.

Stilwell was asked to do the impossible in China. Not unnaturally, he
failed. In his obituary for Stilwell,
General Marshall summarised Stilwell's dilemma aptly:

'He was out at the end of the thinnest
supply line of all. . . . He had a most
difficult problem of great distances,
almost impossible terrain, wide-
spread disease and unfavourable
climate; he faced an extremely complex political problem and his purely
military problem of opposing large
numbers of enemy with few resources
was unmatched in any theatre.

'He stood, as it were, the middle
man between two great governments
other than his own with slender resources and problems somewhat over-
whelming in their complexity. As a
consequence, it deemed necessary in
the fall of 1944 to relieve General
Stilwell of the burden of his responsibilities in Asia and give him a
respite from attempting the
impossible.'

Stilwell left China on 27th October
1944. Although forbidden to make any
public statement about his recall by
his superiors, Stilwell's notebook
made available to scholars after his
death in 1946, revealed his assessment
of the events leading to his relief from
command duties in the CBI theatre:
'Given a mission and no means. Ham-
strung by "no bargaining". Three
years of struggle. Secret reports by

Chinese, British, and special emis-
saries – Currie, Willkie, Wallace,
Nelson, Hurley. Command functions
reduced by ATC, XXBC, Fourteenth
AF . . . Bucked by the British. Bucked
by the Chinese.
In spite of it all, just ready to blossom,
and then made whipping dog for CKS.
It was 19th September radio that got
CKS. He blamed it on me – FDR was
his great friend. FDR did not stand up
to it. I was relieved on the arbitrary
stand and false statements of Chiang
Kai-shek.'

The Stilwell affair had important
consequences for Sino-American relations in general and Chennault in
particular. The affair alienated many
American officials and altered the
cause of public opinion in the United
States. Whereas Chennault had enjoyed wide support in the US until the
recall of Stilwell, his reputation was
blemished as a result of his role in the
machinations against Stilwell. More
important, his actions provided his
critics at the War Department with
fuel to use against him. Although
Chennault enjoyed the confidence of
Stilwell's successor, General Wedemeyer, he no longer had the confidence of Wedemeyer's superiors, General Arnold and General Marshall.
Because they believed Chennault's
usefulness was compromised by his
collaboration with Chiang Kai-shek,
he was relieved of his command by the
War Department at the earliest opportunity.

If Chennault's influence at the
Pentagon declined because of the
Stilwell affair, for Chiang Kai-shek,
the effects of the affair were more
profound. His triumph over Stilwell
led him to believe that the United
States was so dependent upon him to
protect its Far Eastern interests that
the United States government would
yield to his demands on most if not all
issues. This misconception proved to
be a fatal miscalculation and contributed ultimately to the downfall
of the Generalissimo.

# Counteroffensive

General Wedemeyer arrived in Chungking to assume his responsibilities as American commander in the China theatre and military adviser to Chiang Kai-shek on 31st October. At the time of his arrival, the Japanese advance into east China was progressing according to schedule with no sign that the Chinese Army or the Flying Tigers would be able to stop the Japanese from overrunning installations of the Fourteenth Air Force or securing all stops along the Hankow-Hanoi railroad. Discord between American officers was rife and Sino-American relations were at a low ebb. Troop morale was declining and combat efficiency decreasing. To overcome these obstacles, heal wounds, and conduct an effective

campaign against the Japanese required a man of great ability, tact, and political acumen. Wedemeyer was such a man.

Unlike his predecessor, Wedemeyer enjoyed the confidence of the Generalissimo and Chennault. He also enjoyed the confidence of the JCS. His role in China, although more restricted than Stillwell's was more realistic. Wedemeyer's primary missions were to assist the Generalissimo in the conduct of the war against the Japanese and to direct American forces, almost exclusively Air Force, in the assistance of the Chinese. Wedemeyer had no duties or obligations in Burma, which was separated from the China theatre after Stilwell's departure, and he was explicitly warned not to employ United States resources for suppression of civil strife or to interfere in any way with domestic Chinese political matters. In short, whereas Stilwell wore many hats, never knowing clearly the limit of his obligations and responsibilities Wedemeyer's mission was precisely defined, leaving little room for doubt as to what his functions were to be.

In so far as the majority of American forces in China were attached to the Fourteenth Air Force, it was imperative that Wedemeyer work cooperatively with the commander of the Flying Tigers, General Chennault, or find a replacement for Chennault if they could not get on. Fortunately for both men, there were no personality conflicts or major conflicts of interest to divide them and they worked well together from the start of Wedemeyer's mission. Their friendship paid dividends to both men. For Wedemeyer, the fact that Chennault supported him wholeheartedly facilitated the development of a warm bond between himself and the Generalissimo, always a strong patron and supporter of Chennault. For Chen-

**Potent addition to a Tiger's armament; informally named P-40 accepts 1,000lb bomb**

Members of the Walkers' Club—airmen
who have had to return from missions
behind Japanese lines on foot

nault, Wedemeyer's confidence and
support led to increased supply and
ground support which enabled his
men to reverse their fortunes in a
matter of months. With an end to the
political back-biting and bickering
in sight, all parties joined forces to
deter the Japanese from moving
further into east China.

The immediate task facing Chennault and Wedemeyer after the
latter's arrival in China was to prevent the Japanese from taking
Kweilin and if that was not possible,
to prepare an adequate defence for
Kunming, headquarters city of the
Fourteenth Air Force. Kweilin was
already under seige when Wedemeyer
arrived and little could be done to
stop the Japanese from capturing the
city. Accordingly, after continuing
the resistance at Kweilin for the first
nine days of November, the aerodrome
was quickly evacuated and the landing strip and other military facilities
which might be useful to the Japanese
were destroyed. The city fell to the
Japanese on 10th November.

After capturing Kweilin, Japanese
forces moved on towards the remaining forward bases of the Fourteenth
Air Force. Liuchow fell on 11th
November and Nanning on 24th
November. By the end of the month,
almost all of the major forward bases
of the Fourteenth Air Force were in
Japanese hands and the communications link between China and Indo-
China was secured. Having accomplished the major goals of Operation
Ichigo, the Japanese were poised to
strike against Kunming, Chungking
and Chengtu.

Although the military situation in
China showed no improvement in
November 1944, there were hopeful
signs that the situation might soon
change. With the opening of the
the Stilwell Road soon to be realised
land-lease supplies and heavy equip-

## Chennault directs defensive operations on the ground

ment would once more flow into China at a regular and rapid pace, thus, facilitating the operations of all Chinese and American units and ending the arguments over allocation of limited resources. Even if this were not realised immediately, the increased tonnage flown over the Hump would permit more aggressive use of manpower and equipment. After two years of effort and labour, ATC operations were showing a marked increase in productivity, due, no doubt, to the completion of air fields in Assam. Although Chennault had lost some of his forward bases, for the first time in the war he was receiving adequate and growing stocks of supplies, replacement parts, and some new equipment. Wedemeyer assembled his lieutenants in Chungking in November 1944

to plan a counteroffensive against the Japanese. After several days of careful deliberation and debate, a complex plan, acceptable to all, emerged. Known as Operation Alpha, the American plan called for a multiphase operation designed to hold the line in front of Kunming and then push the Japanese back until they were forced to relinquish their new acquisitions in east China. Following this, the Americans and their Chinese allies would force their way back into occupied China.

Phase I of Operation Alpha was to begin in December 1944, if the Generalissimo approved of the overall plan. During this part of the operation, Chinese land forces would initiate contacts with the Japanese in south and south-east China, slowing their advance toward Kunming, while American air power would be used to demolish Japanese positions and dis-

138

rupt supply convoys. If all went according to schedule, the Chinese would have bought sufficient time to complete preparations for the defence of Kunming and prepare for the offensive to come.

Phase II of the operation would begin in January 1945 and centre on the approaches to Kunming. To be sure that the Chinese garrison defending the city would be sufficiently strong to prevent the Japanese from taking Kunming, Wedemeyer proposed that Chinese troops in Burma and India be redeployed in China. This would add at least another 87,500 troops, giving the Chinese numerical superiority over the Japanese. Once again, Chennault would support the operation with his air force, hindering the movement of Japanese troops and menacing their supply convoys.

Phase III would begin as soon as the first two phases of the program were completed successfully, probably in the spring of 1945. In this part of the operation, Chennault's Fourteenth Air Force would play a major role, carrying the war back to Japanese occupied China, destroying land communications and interdicting all supply routes. Following the disruption of Japanese shipping, land communication, and troop retreats, Chinese armies would move forward to liberate their country.

The success of Operation Alpha would depend upon two factors: Chiang Kai-shek's willingness to cooperate and contribute the manpower necessary to execute the operation and Chennault's ability to coordinate his operations with those of his colleagues and superiors.

As one of the architects of Operation Alpha, Chennault was prepared to support it fully. After all that had transpired since he first proposed his air plan in 1942, Chennault could hardly maintain that he could single-handedly defeat the Japanese with his air force alone. His bitter experience had taught him otherwise. Moreover, since there was no conflict between Chennault and Wedemeyer, he had no difficulty in accepting Wedemeyer's direction. On the contrary, Chennault was more than willing to cooperate with Wedemeyer because he felt that Wedemeyer, unlike Stilwell, appreciated the potential of air power. Operation Alpha offered Chennault another opportunity to wrest aerial supremacy from the Japanese. He could hardly refuse to take advantage of this opportunity.

For the first time in the history of the China theatre, the American command was unified in support of a common program, an accomplishment of no mean proportion in light of the history of dissent so characteristic of the area command. Together, the Americans sought to sell their program to Chiang Kai-shek.

The Generalissimo's reaction to Project Alpha was favourable to the plan in general but critical of some of the plan's specifics, particularly Wedemeyer's suggestions concerning deployment and command of troops which had been used to contain Chinese Communist forces to the north. Such objections notwithstanding, Chiang gave his assent to the program, although the actual implementation of the plan was delayed several weeks due to arguments within the Chinese command and poor communication between Chungking and some field units. Despite these delays, the operation was launched in late December.

As the Allies moved to prepare for the defence of Kunming and their counteroffensive, all resources were mobilised to support the effort. Although the flow of supplies into China had increased to a wartime high level in the autumn of 1944, none of the tonnage flown over the Hump could be wasted on non-essential operations. One of the first casualties as a result of this policy was the B-29 operation at Chengtu. Chennault had long complained that the B-29s consumed a disproportionately high percentage of

Hump tonnage for a small return on that investment. No one listened to him. The B-29 project, a favourite operation of General Arnold and President Roosevelt, continued to consume fourteen per cent of all tonnage flown over the Hump and this priority was maintained even after the Japanese offensive threatened the very existence of the Fourteenth Air Force and the Nationalist régime. All efforts to force Stilwell to reverse this policy and use his emergency powers to transfer the B-29 stocks to the Fourteenth Air Force failed for reasons discussed in the following chapter. Now, however, the situation was different.

Unlike General Stilwell, Wedemeyer had confidence in the potential of air power and a working relationship with Chennault. Like Chennault, Wedemeyer realised that the B-29 operation was a drain of resources and contributed little to the defence of China. Even before he assumed his command, he had suggested to the JCS that the operation be cancelled. After arriving in China, his feeling about the matter became even stronger. The B-29s would have to go. There could be no justification for continuing the operation in light of the emergency in China. Wedemeyer lost no opportunity to make his view known to his superiors and they finally accepted his judgment, ordering the closing of the B-29 base at Chengtu and the transfer of fuel stocks and supplies to the Fourteenth Air Force in January 1945. Thereafter, the supply quota formerly assigned to the B-29 project would be diverted to the Flying Tigers.

With the diversion of supplies from the B-29 project to the Fourteenth Air Force, Chennault's preparations for the counteroffensive against the Japanese were complete. For the first time in the war, the Fourteenth Air Force possessed numerical parity, if not superiority, over the Japanese in manpower and equipment and sufficient fuel reserves to keep their

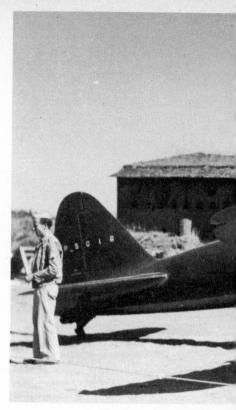

planes in the air. Whereas the Fourteenth Air Force had less than 300 planes at its disposal at the start of the Japanese offensive into east China, on the eve of the new year (1945), the Flying Tigers could muster a force of almost 700 aircraft. Moreover, supplying these planes, which had always been a problem for Chennault, no longer presented difficulties since the total of Hump tonnage received by the Air Force more than doubled during 1944. Thanks to this increase in equipment and supplies, the Flying Tigers were ready to strike back.

Operation Alpha was launched in December 1944. For the men of the Fourteenth Air Force, their activities during this first month of the counteroffensive were quite productive, so much so that Chennault referred to their achievements as 'phenomenal'. Despite the loss of many of their

**Zero captured and pressed into service stands cheek by jowl with more orthodox Flying Tiger**

forward bases, the men of the Fourteenth Air Force successfully carried out a series of raids against Japanese installations at Hankow, Hong Kong, and Nanking from new airfields constructed by the Chinese and several of the old forward bases which the Japanese had never captured. The most notable of these raids was a massive attack on Hankow on 18th December in which Chennault obtained permission to use the B-29s at Chengtu just prior to the departure of the B-29 squadron from China.

The raid on Hankow was one of the largest American air actions in China during the war. 279 planes took part in the raid. When the raid was over, the Wuhan area smouldered for days. Tens of thousands of tons of supplies were destroyed, traffic on the Peiping-Hankow and Hankow-Hanoi railways were disrupted, and dozens of factories were blown up. The raid was so suc-

cessful that Hankow was largely destroyed as a major base of operations for the Japanese. Follow-up raids destroyed whatever facilities had been spared in the 18th December attack.

In January 1945, the Flying Tigers continued to interdict enemy communications, concentrating on the railway lines between Hankow and east China. The purpose of these raids was to cut the flow of supplies to Japanese troops carrying out Operation Ichigo, disrupt the administration of the conquered provinces and to prevent the establishment of an overland line of communication from occupied China to Indo-Chinese ports. By attacking railway installations, bridges and yards, Chennault hoped to

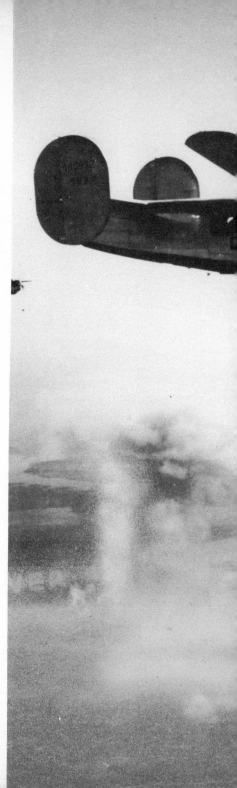

**Shark-nosed Fourteenth AF bomber during successful raid on Japanese installations in Hankow—part of Operation Alpha**

prevent the Japanese from sustaining their offensive and cause the retreat of their armies from east China. Although his men did not accomplish these ends, they did do considerable damage to Japanese supply efforts, reducing the flow of supplies to the front by over fifty per cent. In addition, by destroying at least 142 locomotives and hundreds of box cars, future Japanese supply efforts were severely hampered.

As the men of the Fourteenth Air Force continued their interdiction of Japanese supply convoys in February, the cumulative effects of these raids began to show. Although Japanese troops in east China suffered from no shortage of food, clothing, or ammunition, there was a growing shortage of fuels and lubricants. According to Japanese reports captured after the war, the scarcity of fuel became so acute that it was estimated that all fuel stocks would be consumed by May or June 1945. This led some high ranking Japanese officers to the conclusion that if the situation could not be remedied, the Japanese might be forced to withdraw from China south of the Yangtze. Unknown to Chennault, his counteroffensive was fast proving far more damaging than he had imagined.

The success of Chennault's interdiction raids forced the Japanese to attempt to curtail the activities of the Fourteenth Air Force by capturing their remaining bases in east China. Since the Japanese had far fewer planes than the Americans and could not hope to counter effectively the Flying Tigers in the air, a ground assault on Chennault's bases seemed the only logical alternative to disaster. Such an attack was launched late in January 1945.

The target of the Japanese attack was the Suichuan airfield, head-

**Hankow waterfront after the strike**

quarters of the East China Air Task Force (ECATF) of the Fourteenth Air Force, and other fields in the area. These bases, located hundreds of miles from Fourteenth Air Force headquarters at Kunming, were behind Japanese lines and defended only by the remnants of Hsueh Yueh's army, a motley collection of 150,000 survivors of the Battle of Hengyang. Poorly equipped, hungry, and without ammunition, these forces could hardly put up an adequate defence against the Japanese unless they were supplied from the air or reinforced on the ground. Since Hseuh Yueh was out of favour with the Generalissimo, it was unlikely that Chiang would send a

column to relieve his forces or supply ammunition and new equipment for his army. With no aid in sight, it would be only a matter of time before the Japanese captured the remaining bases of the Fourteenth Air Force and terminated the activities of the ECATF.

Hoping to save the ECATF, Chennault asked Wedemeyer to obtain arms for Hsueh Yueh. When Wedemeyer failed to persuade the Generalissimo to release quantities of arms and send them to Suichuan, Chennault appealed directly to the Generalissimo's associates. From them he learned that no aid would be forthcoming unless Marshal Hsueh was willing to completely subordinate himself to Chiang. Even if he were

late to do any good. It was only after the loss of Suichuan airfield in February that the Chungking government announced the release of equipment and supplies for Hsueh's army. By that time the ECATF had withdrawn from its east China bases to join other units of the Fourteenth Air Force at 'safe' installations. Like some of his predecessors, Chennault saw his military plans sacrificed for political gain, only this time he was not the beneficiary of the Generalissimo's machinations.

With the loss of the remaining bases in east China, Chennault had to revise his plans. However, the Japanese victory at Suichuan in no way ended the American counteroffensive. In that sense, it was a hollow triumph. At the very most, the Japanese set Chennault's time-table back a little but accomplished little else. The interdiction of communications and supply convoys continued but from different bases and the Japanese supply problem worsened accordingly. Unless a new solution to the same problem could be found by the Japanese, they still faced the real possibility that they would have to withdraw their forces north of the Yangtze.

In March, the Fourteenth Air Force carried the counteroffensive into north China, attacking military installations and supply depôts along the Yellow River. In part, this new series of attacks was dictated by the location of new fields constructed by the Chinese for the Fourteenth Air Force to replace fields lost to the Japanese, but, in larger measure, the decision to move the counteroffensive into north China was the result of Chinese Intelligence reports which indicated that damaged railway equipment was being repaired at shops and yards in the north. Accordingly, Chennault focused his attacks on rail repair facilities near Shih-Chia-Chuang, Anyang, Tsinan, and Chenghsien. By the end of the month, these facilities were forced to close

willing to do this, there would be no guarantee that the Generalissimo would come to his rescue. After all, if Hsueh were to win a victory over the Japanese, his increased stature might provide Chiang with some competition. Considering Hsueh's reputation for ambitiousness and the political climate in Chung, the Generalissimo might well let Hsueh Yueh go down to defeat to save his own political future.

Chennault's only alternative was to persuade Hsueh Yueh to humble himself before the Generalissimo, a most difficult task in light of the marshal's temperament. That Chennault was able to succeed in persuading Hsueh to submit to Chiang was a minor diplomatic miracle which, unfortunately, was accomplished too

**Further 'Alpha' missions are aimed at Japanese supply points and communications**

down or drastically curtail activities. The disruption of rail supply efforts was almost complete.

Although the interdiction of communication and supply lines received first priority by the Flying Tigers, where circumstances and resources permitted, attacks on Japanese shipping in China, Indo-China, and Hong Kong continued. These attacks further complicated the problem of supply for the Japanese who now faced a situation in which it was nearly impossible to move supplies and men into or through China whether by rail, truck convoy, or ship. Unless another attempt was made to neutralise the Fourteenth Air Force, all Japanese activities in China would soon grind to a halt.

In order to break the supply bottleneck the Japanese launched a second offensive against the Fourteenth Air Force on 10th April 1945. Concentrating their attack against American air fields at Chihchiang, the Japanese hoped to neutralise the Fourteenth Air Force in central China, gain control of the vital Hsiang valley, gateway to Chungking and Kunming, and advance toward the wartime capital, forcing the Allies to interrupt Operation Alpha and the interdiction campaign of the Flying Tigers. To accomplish these goals, the Japanese massed an army of 60,000 men and a small air unit of several irregular fighter squadrons.

Japanese preparations for the

**Loading with .50-calibre ammunition for a strafing raid**

Chinese army unit moves to prepare a defensive position against expected attack

**Fourteenth AF personnel fuse 500-lb bombs**

offensive in the Hsiang valley did not go unnoticed by Allied reconnaissance planes and Intelligence units. Thus, as the Japanese moved men into position to begin their three-pronged attack on the air bases at Chihchiang, the Chinese and Americans made appropriate preparations to defend against the Japanese offensive.

Chinese forces in the area of the Chihchiang bases numbered approximately 100,000 men. This gave the Allies an almost two to one advantage in manpower. In the past such numerical advantages had meant little to the Chinese in light of the superior

equipment, training, and morale of their Japanese adversaries. However, in this case, the situation was different. The Chinese armies in the Hsiang valley were comparatively well equipped and supplied and some of the troops had been trained under American auspices. More important, the commander of Chinese forces in the area, General Wang Yao-wu, was on good terms with the Generalissimo and there was no chance that his efforts would suffer because of political considerations. No effort would be spared to insure his victory over the Japanese. Thus, all in all, the Chinese were in a good position to resist the Japanese advance.

Cooperating closely with the Four-

**Flying Tigers have command in the air—
their final effort dashes Japanese hopes**

teenth Air Force, the Chinese were able to repulse the Japanese attack in one of the first truly coordinated air-to-ground actions of the war in China. For two months, the Chinese and Americans, coordinating their efforts through air-to-ground liason teams, held the Japanese in check. While the Chinese held the Japanese back on the ground, the Flying Tigers attacked them from the air dropping napalm bombs from diving fighters and firing millions of rounds of ammunition. There was little the Japanese could do to protect themselves from these anti-personnel weapons and, as a consequence, they suffered heavy casualties.

The Japanese offensive ended unsuccessfully in June 1945, although as early as 15th May, it was clear that the Japanese had been decisvely defeated at Chihchiang. The effects of the Sino-American victory were immediate. The Japanese were forced to retreat from east China and the Yangtze. With their departure, the danger to the Chungking regime was over. After seven years of war, victory was in sight. For the Chinese the victory marked the beginning of a new era. For Chennault and his Flying Tigers, the victory was their 'last hurrah'.

# The end
# of the road

Ironically, the Fourteenth Air Force did not survive long after its most decisive victory of the war but fell victim to a reorganisation of American forces in China. After spending years in China facing constant danger and overcoming numerous obstacles, neither Chennault nr his Flying Tigers remained there to witness the final victory over Japan.

The plan to reorganise the American air command in China, which ultimately led Chennault to tender his resignation from the Army Air Force, originated with General George Stratemeyer, Chennault's immediate superior in the Air Force, in January 1945. It was based on two considerations: the imminent liberation of Burma and the need to mobilise all Army Air Force resources in Asia in support of American forces in the Pacific as they moved toward the China mainland. With the end of the Burma campaign, the Tenth Air Force would complete its mission in India and could be transferred to China where it would be merged with the Fourteenth Air Force. The en-larged Army Air Force in China resulting from this merger would play a major role in the plan (Project Beta) to establish an Allied beachhead on the China coast, viewed by the JCS as an absolute prerequisite of the final assault on Japan. In so far as the reorganisation of US air resources in Asia would facilitate the achievement of these goals, Stratemeyer's scheme had the support of all involved with American military operations in China and India except for General Chennault.

Chennault was informed of the plan of the JCS to incorporate his Fourteenth Air Force into a larger air command in China in late January 1945, several days after Generals Wedemeyer, Stratemeyer, and Sultan agreed to the merger of the Tenth and Fourteenth Air Forces at a special meeting held at Myitkyina in Burma on 15th January. His immediate reaction to the plan was negative, but in his conversations with Wedemeyer subsequent to the Myitkyina meeting Chennault was outspoken in his criticism of the scheme.

Chennault's opposition to the Stratemeyer plan was based on several factors. Firstly, Chennault did not believe that a build-up of AAF units in China could be justified in light of available logistical support. Secondly, he did not wish to be subordinated to another commander in China after years of managing the air war in China on his own. Since the reorganisation plan did not provide for Chennault to direct the new AAF in China, he balked at accepting an inferior role to General Stratemeyer who had been designated to command the new AAF by the JCS.

Correctly or otherwise, Chennault believed that the reorganisation plan had been devised by his enemies to force his resignation. Although this view was undoubtedly somewhat paranoic, there can be no doubt that

**Bombers are destroyed on the ground by Fourteenth AF fighters**

Chennault's critics were anxious to replace him as commander of the Fourteenth Air Force at the earliest opportunity. The official record confirms this. Even if the reorganisation scheme was not carried out, Chennault would have probably been removed from China before the end of the war. The Stratemeyer scheme simply offered a convenient pretext for his removal, although it was not designed solely with that end in mind.

In the course of his career in China, Chennault had alienated most of his superiors. While they could not deny his ability and accomplishments, they continued to be critical of his unorthodox policies and his insubordination. If General Stilwell had failed to make his mark on Chiang Kai-shek and Roosevelt, Chennault had never made his on General Arnold and General Marshall. In the end, this proved costly to the commander of the Flying Tigers.

As preparations for the Beta Plan went ahead, it was decided that Chennault would only be an obstacle in the path of achieving a victory over the Japanese and would have to be removed. This view was bluntly expressed to General Wedemeyer by General Arnold in June 1945. In a letter to the commander of American forces in the China theatre, Arnold made the following observation about Chennault:

'General Chennault has been in China for a long period of time fighting a defensive air war with minimum resources. The meagreness of supplies and the resulting guerilla type of warfare must change to a modern type of striking, offensive air power. I firmly believe that the quickest and most effective way to change air warfare in your Theatre, employing modern offensive thought, tactics and techniques, is to change commanders. I would appreciate your concurrence in General Chennault's early with-

**Japanese air bases are given no chance of recovery**

drawal from the Chinese Theatre. He should take advantage of the retirement privileges now available to physically disabled officers that make their pay not subject to Income Tax. Otherwise, he may be reduced and put back on the retired list at his permanent rank.'

Arnold's note and similar memos from General Marshall put Wedemeyer on the spot. It was clear to him that the Joint Chiefs of Staff would not continue to tolerate Chennault's presence in China and would recall him if he did not voluntarily resign his commission, on the other hand, despite his initial hesitation about working with Chennault, Wedemeyer had grown to admire him. Wedemeyer accordingly sought to retain Chennault in the China theatre, proposing that he be allowed to stay on in China as head of the new Strategic Air Force operating under the command

**Creator of the Flying Tigers, now pushed aside as an obstacle to final victory**

**Claire Chennault chooses to resign rather than be fired—the farewell dinner given by Chiang Kai-shek**

of General Stratemeyer. When it became apparent that the JCS would not accept this compromise, Wedemeyer tried to postpone the merger of the Tenth and Fourteenth Air Forces until Chennault could be persuaded to 'bow out gracefully'. Although Wedemeyer supported the reorganisation plan in general, he refused to participate in any plan designed to humiliate Chennault if this could be avoided. Unfortunately, Wedemeyer could do little to spare Chennault the humiliation of leaving the China theatre before the end of the war.

Chennault submitted his request for retirement from the Army Air Force on 6th July 1945. After eight years in China, he prepared to vacate his command rather than be forced to relinquish it. Although grateful for Wedemeyer's support, Chennault left China an angry and bitter man, prevented from witnessing the final victory over

157

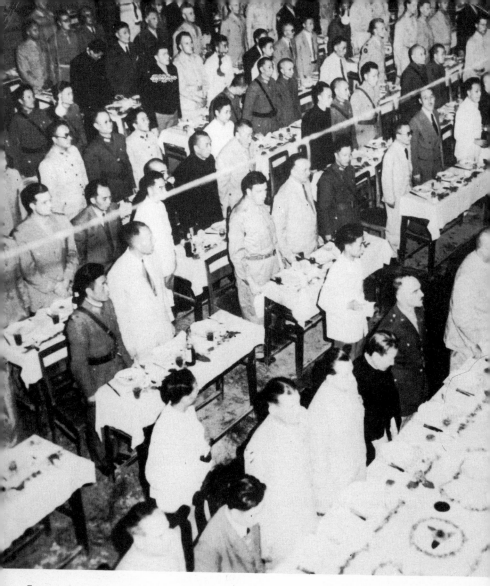

Japan by the partisans of General Stilwell. With his departure, an epoch ended. Although the Fourteenth Air Force continued to serve in China as part of the expanded Army Air Force, the spirit of the Flying Tigers died with the resignation of their commander.

The Flying Tigers neither won nor lost the war in China. By providing aerial protection to the Chinese government and people, they per-

formed a valuable service at a time when no other protection was available. At the same time, however, the aggressive and unorthodox nature of their tactics invited Japanese retaliation and prolonged the war, increasing the losses suffered by the people of Free China. Neither saviours or villains, the members of the Flying Tigers, whether part of the American Volunteer Group, China Air Task Force, nor the Fourteenth Air Force,

appreciation of the potential of air power on the part of General Stilwell would have facilitated the more efficient use of limited resources in China, thereby contributing to a shortening of the war effort. General Wedemeyer proved that a co-ordinated ground and aerial program could succeed after assuming command of American forces in China. That this co-operation was not achieved prior to his mission was the great tragedy of the war in the China-Burma-India theatre.

Looking back over the events and personalities of the war years in the CBI theatre, one is not surprised that the co-operation alluded to above was not achieved until late in the war. Considering the conflicting goals and interests of the major protagonists (Chennault and Stilwell, Chiang Kai-shek and Franklin D Roosevelt, General Marshall and Ambassador T V Soong), there was little possibility of creating a diplomatic and military entente in China. The broad differences between the Chinese and American approaches to and conceptions of the war meant that military and political policies would never coincide exactly. Furthermore such basic differences were complicated by the strong personalities and views of the major actors in the CBI, and it is in this context that the dilemma of the China theatre must be defined.

Chennault and his Flying Tigers were victims of and participants in the complex China tangle. They could neither reshape it nor escape it. Therein lay the root of their problems. Their contribution to the war effort was influenced by events over which they had no immediate control. Such being the case, their role was a limited one. However exciting or romantic, neither Chennault nor his Flying Tigers performed any definitive feat in the CBI. They simply facilitated the inevitable.

performed a necessary function in a war theatre limited by lack of commitment, leadership, manpower, and resources. They accomplished no more and no less.

There is little evidence to indicate that air power alone could have won the war in China. The records clearly substantiate this fact and negate Chennault's wartime and postwar arguments. On the other hand, it is also clear that a more adequate

# Bibliography

*A Military History of Modern China 1924-1949* by F F Liu (Princeton University Press)

*Stilwell and the American Experience in China* by Barbara Tuchman (Macmillan, New York)

*Stilwell's Command Problems* by C Romanus and R Sunderland (Department of the Army, Washington)

*Stilwell's Mission to China* by C Romanus and R Sunderland (Department of ᵗʰᵉ Army, Washington)

*The China Tangle* by Herbert Feis (Princeton University Press)

*The Stilwell Papers* by Joseph W Stilwell (Sloane, New York)

*The United States Army Air Forces in World War II* by Wesley F Craven and James Lea Cate (eds) (University of Chicago Press)

*United States Relations with China (China White Paper)* (Department of State, Washington)

*Way of a Fighter: the Memoirs of Claire Lee Chennault* by Claire Chennault (Putnam, New York)

*Wedemeyer Reports* by Albert Wedemeyer (Holt, New York)